# WOLDS
# WAY

# WOLDS WAY

## Roger Ratcliffe

*Photographs by Ian Carstairs*
*General editor Michael Allaby*

AURUM PRESS

COUNTRYSIDE COMMISSION · ORDNANCE SURVEY

## ACKNOWLEDGEMENTS

I wish to recognise the Ramblers' Association, East Yorkshire and Derwent Area, which first conceived the idea of a Wolds Way, and the footpath officers of Humberside County Council and North Yorkshire County Council, whose hard work made it a reality. These groups also helped me with my research.

Roger Ratcliffe was formerly Environment Correspondent of the *Yorkshire Post* and North of England Correspondent of the *Sunday Times*. He currently runs his own publishing business.

This edition first published 1992 by Aurum Press Ltd in association with the Countryside Commission and the Ordnance Survey
Text copyright © 1992 by Aurum Press Ltd, the Countryside Commission and the Ordnance Survey
Maps Crown copyright © 1992 by the Ordnance Survey
Photographs copyright © 1992 by the Countryside Commission

British Library Cataloguing in Publication Data
Ratcliffe, Roger
Wolds Way. – (National trail guides; 14)
1. Walking recreations. Humberside (England). North Yorkshire (England)
I. Title II. Allaby, Michael, 1933– III. Ordnance Survey
IV. Great Britain. *Countryside Commission* V. Series
914.283

ISBN 1 85410 189 7
OS ISBN 0 319 00236 5

Book design by Robert Updegraff
Cover photograph: a characteristic Wolds landscape near Huggate Sheepwalk
Title page photograph: a typical Wolds chalk valley, near Wharram Percy

Typeset by Wyvern Typesetting Ltd, Bristol
Printed and bound in Italy by Printers Srl, Trento

# Contents

Circular walks appear on pages 48, 69, 94, 112 and 126

# How to use this guide

This guide to the 79-mile (127-kilometre) Wolds Way is in three parts:

- The introduction, with an historical background to the area and advice for walkers.
- The Way itself, split into five chapters, with maps opposite the description for each route section. The distances noted with each chapter represent the total length of the Wolds Way, including sections through towns and villages. This part of the guide also includes information on places of interest as well as a number of short walks that can be taken around parts of the path. Key sites are numbered both in the text and on the maps to make it easier to follow the route description.
- The last part includes useful information such as local transport, accommodation and organisations involved with the Wolds Way.

The maps have been prepared by the Ordnance Survey for this trail guide using 1:25 000 Pathfinder or Outdoor Leisure maps as a base. The line of the Wolds Way is shown in yellow, with the status of each section of the trail – footpath or bridle-way, for example – shown in green underneath (see key on inside front cover). These rights of way markings also indicate the precise alignment of the Wolds Way, which you should follow. In some cases, the yellow line on these maps may show a route that is different from that shown on older maps; you are recommended to follow the yellow route in this guide, which will be the route that is waymarked with the distinctive acorn symbol ● used for all national trails. Any parts of the Wolds Way that may be difficult to follow on the ground are clearly highlighted in the route description, and important points to watch for are marked with letters in each chapter, both in the text and on the maps. *Some maps start on a right-hand page and continue on the left-hand page – black arrows ( ➤ ) at the edge of the maps indicate the start point.*

Should there be a need to divert the Wolds Way from the route shown in this guide, for maintenance work or because the route has had to be changed, you are advised to follow any waymarks or signs along the path.

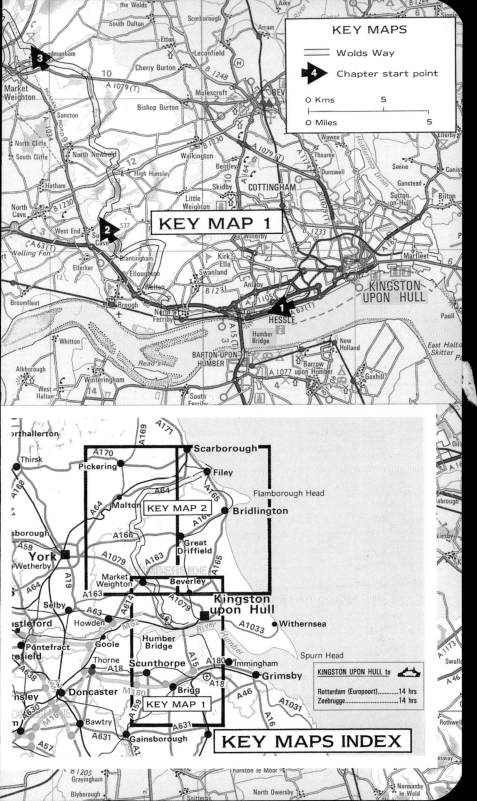

KEY MAPS

Wolds Way

4  Chapter start point

0 Kms                    5

0 Miles                  5

KEY MAP 1

KEY MAP 2

KEY MAP 1

KEY MAPS INDEX

KINGSTON UPON HULL to

Rotterdam (Europoort)............14 hrs
Zeebrugge...............................14 hrs

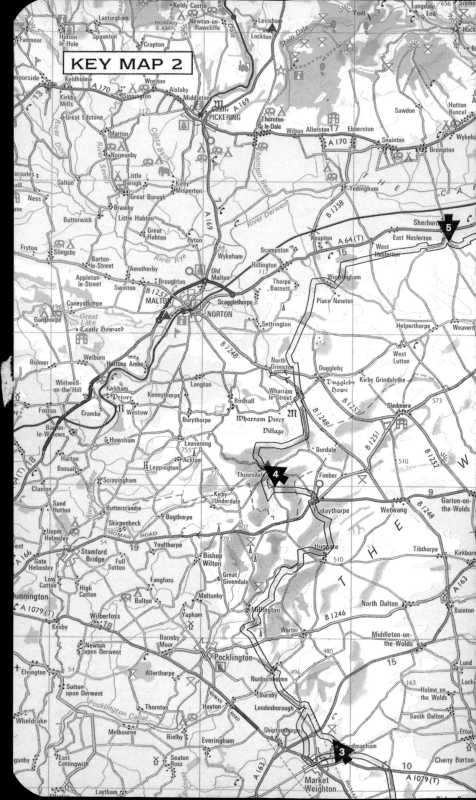

*Skidby Mill, near Beverley, the last surviving windmill to be found in the north-east.*

## Distance checklist

This list will assist you in calculating the distances between your proposed overnight accommodation and in checking your progress along the walk.

| location | approx. distance from previous location | |
|---|---|---|
| | miles | km |
| Hessle | 0 | 0 |
| North Ferriby | 3.1 | 5.0 |
| Welton | 3.5 | 5.6 |
| Brantingham | 4.2 | 6.7 |
| South Cave | 2.1 | 3.4 |
| Newbald | 5.2 | 8.4 |
| Goodmanham | 5.8 | 9.3 |
| (Market Weighton – from Newbald) | (6.7) | (10.8) |
| Londesborough | 2.4 | 3.9 |
| (Londesborough – from Market Weighton) | (2.7) | (4.3) |
| Nunburnholme | 2.5 | 4.0 |
| Millington | 2.7 | 4.3 |
| Huggate | 5.9 | 9.5 |
| Fridaythorpe | 2.5 | 4.0 |
| Thixendale | 4.1 | 6.6 |
| Wharram le Street | 5.3 | 8.5 |
| Settrington Beacon | 3.7 | 6.0 |
| Wintringham | 2.7 | 4.3 |
| Sherburn | 6.8 | 10.9 |
| Ganton | 3.0 | 4.8 |
| Staxton Wold | 3.2 | 5.1 |
| Muston | 6.5 | 10.5 |
| Filey | 1.5 | 2.4 |
| Cleveland Way | 2.7 | 4.3 |

# PREFACE

National trails are an enticement. Every time I see a new one on the map I want to walk it. They will lead you out into your countryside on a natural line. Some of the upland paths are rooted in our history: the 'green roads' of England.

Trails like the Wolds Way are particularly suited for long journeys, but they can also be tried out on an afternoon or over a weekend. Or use them as part of a round trip, or circular walk; suggestions for these are included in this guide. National trails are maintained by local authorities on behalf of the Commission, and are well waymarked with our distinctive acorn. Each trail provides a good, and sometimes challenging, walk or ride in the countryside.

I hope that you will go and make the most of them, using this guide to keep you on the correct route and to add to your enjoyment of the countryside and understanding of the area.

John Johnson
Chairman
Countryside Commission

PART ONE

# INTRODUCTION

It is ironic that lovers of unspoilt countryside in northern England often eschew national parks like the Yorkshire Dales and North York Moors. Instead, they find peace and quiet and spiritual renewal in the Yorkshire Wolds, where no Act of Parliament has been necessary to safeguard the landscape's essential character. These gently rolling chalk hills with their wooded slopes and deep green, almost secretive, valleys have avoided the coffee-table book treatment. Few coach parties hog their narrow lanes, crocodiles of walkers are rarely met on the springy footpaths, and the pretty, pantile-roofed houses in Wolds villages are not second homes or holiday cottages.

There is no better way to discover the many historic and picturesque gems in these hills than by following the Wolds Way along its 79 miles (127 km). From Hessle Haven, beside the gritty brown Humber, to the airy cliffs above Filey, the national trail links virtually all of the interesting features to be found in this last great thrust of English chalk. There is the mighty Humber Bridge, the longest single-span in the world; there are wonderful abandoned railway lines to walk along, or the route of England's oldest horse race; the best-preserved deserted medieval village is at Wharram Percy; and the most fascinating geological curiosity on the English coast is Filey Brigg, climax of the Wolds Way.

In between, there are beautiful woodland walks, bracing field tops with breathtaking views and the dry chalk valleys that have remained largely unchanged for centuries.

It is a landscape that has been described as 'a piece of southern England in the North', for it is difficult to imagine a greater contrast with the exposed heather moors, wild peaty bogs and gritstone fells that one associates with northern England. Being mostly Grade 1 agricultural land, there is no reason to fear that these splendid chalk downs will ever be encroached upon by developments like new towns and industrial estates. Even a major north–south privately built motorway, proposed for the late 1990s, would skirt the western edge and come close to the Wolds Way only at Market Weighton.

The Wolds Way demands the use of tarmac lanes at many places but these lanes, most of them rarely used by traffic, are an essential feature of the hills, and walkers should relish them as such. Most have very wide grass verges, since they were old drove roads, making walking both safe and comfortable.

All the walks described in this book will appeal to every level of walking ability. There are short sections, and longer ones for those who like to cover a lot of ground. One thing is certain – even the most accomplished of national trail walkers, perhaps with fresh memories of the wilder sections of Offa's Dyke or the ancient Ridgeway, will not fail to be seduced by the placid Wolds countryside.

## The Wolds Way story

The formation of long-distance footpaths in England and Wales was very much a product of the 1960s expansion of leisure time, disposable income and interest in the countryside. Following the Pennine Way's opening in 1965, there was pressure from ramblers for a number of other routes that would traverse a range of hills while linking a series of historic and scenic treasures.

*An autumn sight – hawthorn berries along the Wolds Way.*

The Wolds Way was one such continuous footpath. The idea came from the Ramblers' Association, East Yorkshire and Derwent Area, whose members had long appreciated the beauties of the Yorkshire Wolds. Their proposal was put to the National Parks Commission (forerunner of the Countryside Commission) in 1967 and within a year it had been approved in principle by the new Commission and by the East Riding County Council. The route would begin on the Humber shore at North Ferriby and finish at the East Riding county boundary just north of Filey Brigg.

The first section to open was a 4-mile (6.5-km) path through Goodmanham and Londesborough, which was officially inaugurated by Lord Halifax, then Lord Lieutenant of the East Riding, in November 1973. But it was not until 26th July 1977 that the Countryside Commission formally proposed a complete route. It had taken 10 years to get just one small stretch of the national trail officially opened and waymarked; it was to take another five years to get agreement over the rest of the Wolds Way.

The route that was finally agreed included an extension to Hessle Haven, at its southernmost end, and a link with Market Weighton. The most difficult sections to secure were at the northern end, between Thixendale and Filey, and about 10 miles of new rights of way had to be created. At last, the official route was opened on 2nd October 1982, at a ceremony performed by a major Wolds landowner, Lord Middleton, at Fridaythorpe.

## Chalk landscape

Chalk underlies virtually all of the Wolds Way. Only the final stretch of walking on the boulder clay cliffs north from Filey, and the anomalous black reef of lower calcareous gritstone that forms Filey Brigg, provide a contrast in scenery.

The Yorkshire Wolds are, in fact, the northernmost extremity of a continuous band of chalk extending from South Devon. It rolls through Dorset, eastward to form such national landmarks as the Seven Sisters and the White Cliffs of Dover, then ripples through Sussex and Kent as the North and South Downs, dipping under the Thames and London. It also thrusts through Wiltshire and Berkshire and the Chilterns of Buckinghamshire, reaching through Norfolk but again disappearing from view at The Wash to reappear as the Lincolnshire Wolds.

Cut by the mighty Humber, the chalk finally emerges to create the Yorkshire Wolds before terminating as the scenic *pièce de résistance* of Flamborough Head and the high-rise sea-bird colonies of Bempton Cliffs.

Chalk was formed between 65 and 140 million years ago and is composed of the bones and shells of countless minute creatures that accumulated when earth movements reduced the sea level over the infant British landscape. The white mud compressed and hardened, and was squeezed and eroded by volcanic action and the creation of new rivers. The final polish of softly rounded hills and dry valleys was provided by the last Ice Age. And the rest of what we know today as classic English chalk downland scenery was formed by people – the sweet chalk pastures, the steep meadow banks, the well-cultivated and grazed terrain of some of the most fertile land in Europe.

Water is quickly absorbed by chalk, which means that conditions underfoot are never wet for long because the land quickly dries out after rain. This absorption also deprives the landscape of many springs and water courses. A curious characteristic of chalk downland is the streams that usually run underground but occasionally break to the surface. In the Yorkshire Wolds they are known as 'races', the best-known being the Gypsey Race, which runs from Duggleby, just off the Wolds Way, to Bridlington. In southern and western England they are known as 'bournes'. However, in this part of the country water abstraction has meant that the 'races' are a much rarer sight now than they once were.

## History

Some of the oldest cultivated landscape is to be found in chalk downs. Mesolithic tribes from the Continent arrived in southern England as the ice sheets melted and spread north. They lived off the fish and wild animals to be found in the Vale of Pickering to the north of the Wolds.

Around the year 3250 BC came yet more invaders from the Mediterranean who brought with them the earliest farming skills. They had no need for the hunting grounds of marshes but colonised the fertile hills, developing a patchwork of small fields. Thus the Wolds, which have so few habitations today, were very much alive 4,000 years ago. Later settlers arrived from France, tribes of warriors with chieftains whose remains were buried with chariots in great barrows – their main legacy to today's landscape.

*Looking north-east, across the Wolds from above Nunburnholme.*

The Romans arrived in about AD 71. Their principal camp was west of the Wolds at *Eboracum*, the embryonic city of York. They also built a signal station above Filey Brigg, at the end of the Wolds Way, to raise the alarm should the Angles invade from the sea. Indeed, the Angles did just that in the 5th century, but by then the Romans had finished with Britain.

The Saxons, and later the Danes, laid the foundation for much of what you see in the Wolds today – names like Brantingham and Goodmanham are Saxon, while the numerous villages and farm names ending in 'by' and 'thorpe' are a reminder of the Danes. It is thought that many field boundaries, still in use, were first laid out by these pre-Conquest settlers.

Early medieval times were a turbulent period in the area's history. Many people were driven off the land by the Norman barons. The Black Death also caused thousands of casualties and virtually wiped out some settlements, the most famous being Wharram Percy. Later, land enclosures meant that the Wolds were turned over to sheep rearing. Cereal growing, which is the dominant agricultural activity today, began in the 18th century, and since that time hedges may have been grubbed out to enlarge a field but, essentially, you see the same type of landscape that existed 200 years ago.

## Farming

The Yorkshire Wolds is one of the most intensively farmed areas of Britain. About 95 per cent of the land is arable, the main production being cereal crops, such as winter and spring/winter barley. About one-third of the Wolds comprises grazing pastures or oilseed rape production, with a smaller acreage devoted to pea vining. In the 1980s the Wolds became one of Britain's largest producers of oilseed rape.

The soil quality, although good throughout the Wolds, is richest on the southernmost slopes fronting the Humber. The loam is medium to heavy, and the presence of large numbers of chalk stones and pebbles keeps it well drained.

Although the days of the vast sheep walks have long gone, the principal livestock is still sheep. Up to 200,000 lambs and ewes are herded, with most of the common breeds being represented. The Wolds are also used for dairy and beef cattle production, and the predominant breeds are black and white Friesian and Holstein with a few herds of Charolais and Limousin.

*The fine Norman doorway of St Nicholas Church, situated in the village of North Newbald.*

*Forestry work under way in Deepdale Plantation, which lies above the village of Wintringham.*

There are some extremely large farms in the Yorkshire Wolds. These were created during the land enclosures of 1750–1850. Smaller farmsteads exist only beside the villages.

Because the Wolds Way runs almost entirely across agricultural land, it is necessary to be meticulous in your observance of the Country Code (see the inside of the back cover). In particular, you should keep to footpaths, walk in single file in fields where there are crops, be extremely careful with matches or cigarette ends, keep dogs on leads, close all gates behind you, not tamper with machinery, and not pick or destroy crops. Several stretches of the Wolds Way were created with the consent and co-operation of farmers and you should repay them by behaving responsibly.

## Wildlife

Geology is usually the key to an area's wildlife, and chalk downland has some of the most distinctive flora and fauna in the British landscape. Well-drained banks and fields with calcium-rich soils in areas like the Yorkshire Wolds provide ideal conditions for flowers that require lime for their survival, such as harebells, bee orchids, cowslips, buttercups, shepherd's purse, wild thyme and wild basil.

These, in turn, attract colourful butterflies in summer, like the orange tip, red admiral and the common blue. The uncultivated grasses provide nesting places for skylarks, the seeds of tall grasses are food for goldfinches. There are bank voles, which, of course, attract the kestrel, and stoats and weasels lurk in the hedge bottoms. The open fields have hares, partridges, lapwings, yet more musical skylarks, meadow-pipits, and noisy flocks of rooks, gulls and jackdaws appear when the earth is being ploughed.

The hawthorn hedgerows that accompany the Wolds Way for so many miles have their own special inhabitants. All of the common small birds are present throughout the year, as well as family groups of long-tailed tits and the occasional raiding sparrowhawk. Blood-red poppies thrive in the difficult corners out of reach of the plough and, if you rest awhile at a field gate, it is possible you might see a little owl.

The beech woodland sections are often fragrant with honeysuckle, while forget-me-nots, red campion, bluebells and primroses carpet the floor in season. Where the footpath joins a metalled lane, the banks are piled with cow parsley in summer. The woodland and some hedge banks also contain a number of fungi in late summer and autumn, but be warned that most of them are poisonous and the best advice is that, unless you know the subject, leave them alone!

The start and finish of the Wolds Way provide their own distinctive wildlife showcases. On the Humber foreshore there are many wading birds and feeding ducks, while the Yorkshire coast supports most species of British seabirds and, if your skills at bird identification are up to it, many irregular visitors on migration.

## Planning your walk

Virtually the only decision you need to make before you set off from home, if it is your intention to complete the Wolds Way, is in which direction you should walk. There is no reason why, if it appeals to you, you should not begin on the cliffs north of Filey and walk south to just east of the Humber Bridge at Hessle, but there are some good reasons for beginning at the Humber and ending on the coast. One is that it is usually better to walk with the sun on your back, especially on bright days when walking towards it can be dazzling and something of a strain on the eyes. Another south–north justification is to do with the landscape itself. From its inauspicious beginnings on the muddy Humber bank, the beauty of the scenery intensifies by the day. There can be no better finale than Filey Brigg and the gleaming chalk of Flamborough Head seen across Filey Bay. This book describes the route from south to north.

The Wolds Way is not one of the 'heavyweights' of long-distance walking in Britain and even a novice should accomplish it with ease. At no point is the terrain difficult; indeed, with the exception of about half a dozen short inclines where the path climbs out of chalk dales on to the airy Wolds, the whole of the route is on level valley bottoms or open fields.

The route is described in five chapters, each one terminating where accommodation can be found. The first (Hessle to South Cave) covers approximately 13 miles (21 km) in length, which should be just enough if you have driven or travelled by train from home that same day. Public transport provision at the start of the footpath and on the final section makes it possible to do these walks and return to your starting point on the same day. But the stages in between are across areas where rural transport provision is poor and these sections are best done (unless you are with a friend and arrange a transport pick-up at the end) as part of the continuous route.

If you estimate walking at a pace that covers 3 miles (5 km) an hour, your morning start on the sections between Market Weighton and Filey should be no later than 9 a.m. if you wish to arrive at your lodgings in time for an evening meal.

Having decided on your programme, it is wise to book your accommodation in advance (see page 133 for accommodation details).

Overall, the Wolds Way is perfect for a week's holiday. If you start from home on Monday morning, for example, you can easily cover the distance as described in this book by Friday teatime and, after a night's rest, return on the Saturday.

It is best to do the walk in spring, summer or autumn – all have their own special magic. Winter, apart from being scenically rather dull, has the added disadvantage of fewer accommodation options, as many bed and breakfast guesthouses operate only from Easter to October, and public transport can be even harder to find.

## Waymarking

Because of the great need to keep to paths on agricultural land, the footpath is well signposted, especially at junctions with other rights of way and at roads. The signposts are clearly marked 'Wolds Way' and bear the Countryside Commission's national trail symbol, a stylised acorn. The acorn is used in other places where confirmation of the correct path is required. Ignore the small arrows that appear in some places – these refer to local walks that sometimes join the Wolds Way.

## Weather

It is well known that eastern England enjoys lower rainfall than the west side, but that is little consolation to the walker whose long-planned holiday on the Wolds Way coincides with a period of unremitting downpours. However, the weather records of the region do offer a limited guide to anyone making some advance arrangements for a week on the footpath. April, May and June are generally drier than July and August, then in September and October there are often many days of unbroken fine weather. Between November and Easter the Wolds can suffer some of the deepest snowdrifts in England, when the wind turns to the east and cuts like a scythe.

The contrast between Wolds weather and that found on the coast can sometimes be quite remarkable. On scorching days inland, the seaside can be often cooled by sea breezes, which

*The winter snowfields that often cut off Huggate from the outside world.*

also produce cloudy skies. Also on the coast, sea-frets (wet mists coming inland from the sea) gather on windless days when the air is warmer than the sea. These can move onshore and in these circumstances extra care is required if walking on the cliffs above Filey.

Immediately before setting out on the Wolds Way, it might be useful to check the area's weather by telephoning the 24-hour pre-recorded forecast for Lincolnshire and Humberside (covering most of the route). Telephone 0898 500413. There is also a national 5-day forecast on 0898 500400.

## Equipment

In guides to other national trails this section might begin with advice such as 'a good pair of walking boots is essential' but, in the case of the Wolds Way, there are no sections of footpath where they are absolutely essential. The route lies entirely across agricultural land, much of it on gently undulating fields, and the only point at which you could conceivably require a firm grip is the descent to Filey Brigg and the sometimes slimy surface of the Brigg itself. A pair of lightweight walking boots is adequate. They offer some degree of protection on slippery surfaces and will not feel like lead weights after the first day's walk.

*Ripening barley along the western escarpment of the Wolds Way.*

A possible alternative could be a pair of training shoes that you do not mind getting a bit mud-spattered, and a pair of lightweight wellies. The latter are especially useful after rain, when some sections of the footpath are muddy – the wellies are easily washed at the next large puddle! Take several pairs of socks and, since long-distance walking puts considerable strain on your feet, wear a soft, inner pair and a harder outer pair to allow the feet's perspiration to be well absorbed.

Whenever you choose to walk, waterproofs are essential, and their effectiveness depends on what you can afford to buy. Breathable fabrics like Gore-tex, while costly, stop you feeling as if you are walking inside a plastic bin-liner. The once-obligatory extra sweater is now often replaced by a garment in one of the fleecy, ultra-insulating materials on the market. Outside the summer season it is best to take gloves and warm headwear. The best overall advice is to be prepared for the rain and the cold.

Since there are few refreshment stops *en route*, you should take a flask or water bottle and fill it with your requirements before setting out each day. Most farms encountered along the route have outdoor water taps, but ask first before using them.

Do not forget the items that you hope never to need. It is not a waste of time lugging a few emergency tools in your rucksack. Place them in a convenient pocket or position for quick access. Essentials are a compass, in case you stray off the path in mist or darkness; a torch and whistle, which can be used to give the International Distress Signal in an emergency; a small first-aid kit; some high-energy food such as glucose, mint cake, dried fruit or chocolate; a survival bag, especially if walking alone, in case you accidentally fall on a remote stretch of the path; and some hay-fever medication in spring and summer, if you are a sufferer.

## Safety precautions

The Wolds Way has been divided into five different sections in this book and each one should be within the abilities of the average walker carrying a rucksack of around 30 lb (14 kg). Between the overnight stops, villages and houses are rare, so make sure that you are equipped for any emergency.

There are only a few parts of the footpath where slips or falls might occur. These are on some of the steep banks climbing out of the chalk dales, such as Rabbit Warren and Nettle Dale, near Millington; the ascent of Deep Dale from Wintringham; or

*The old lifeboat station at Coble Landing, Filey. The lifeboat is towed to and from the sea by tractor.*

at Filey Brigg and the nearby cliffs. However, only carelessness could result in an accident.

The path along the Humber foreshore at North Ferriby is liable to flooding at the time of high spring tides, but a safe alternative is described in this book. If you wish to explore Filey Brigg, check the state of the tide (ask at the tourist information centre in John Street, Filey) and avoid it altogether when the tide is high. You should also bypass it if a sea-fret blankets the coast. Along the cliff footpath, do not stray too near the edge. If you want to get a wide view of the coast use the good, safe vantage points.

If you do have an emergency, look in this guide book for the location of the nearest farm, telephone box or village. If you are able to send someone to raise the alarm, give this book to that person, once they have established your exact location.

In extreme circumstances, you may need to employ the International Distress Signal using a torch or whistle. This is six long flashes or blasts in quick succession, repeated at one-minute intervals.

PART TWO

# WOLDS WAY

# 1 Hessle to South Cave

*via North Ferriby and Welton*
*13 miles (20.9 km)*

For those walkers travelling from home to reach the beginning of the Wolds Way and thus getting a late start on the footpath, this opening section should be easily completed in time to reach overnight accommodation and an evening meal at a reasonable hour. Until Welton is reached it is level walking although, on a fine day, you will not wish to hurry the 3-mile (5-km) stretch that partners the fascinating Humber estuary **1** (see page 42).

The national trail begins opposite the Ferryboat Inn, on the west side of Hessle Haven. If you arrive by train, take the railway bridge south from Hessle Station and turn left on Redcliff Road. Those given a lift to the start (it is not advisable to leave a vehicle parked overnight at the car park) should leave the Clive Sullivan Way at the Hessle turn-off and follow the sign for Livingstone Road.

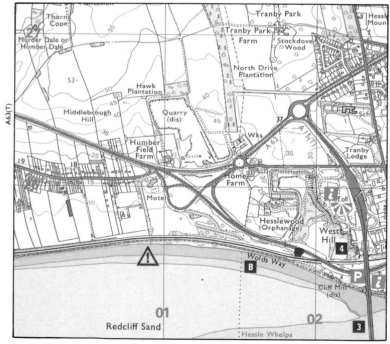

Contours are given in metres
The vertical interval is 5m

Take the signposted path **A** opposite Richard Dunston's boatyard **2** down to the Humber estuary and turn right past the large picnic area towards a scene dominated by the Humber Bridge **3** (see page 43). Evidence that this is the start of chalk downland abounds – just look at the white pebbles and rocks on the beach. The noise of oxyacetylene torches and riveting guns from the boatyard may follow you along the shore – this is the sole survivor of an industry that has existed on the Humber for more than 400 years.

The area around the bridge contains many car parking spaces and visitor facilities, including information boards explaining the Humber's history and wildlife. Once under the giant legs (510 ft/156 metres high with foundations 26 ft/ 8 metres deep) you will see the frontage of the Humber Bridge Country Park **4**, which includes the ruin of an old five-sail windmill. The park was established around a chalk quarry and opened in 1986.

Continuing west through the swing gate on to the pebble beach **B**, the path has the Humber on the left and the Hull– Selby railway line (opened on 2nd July 1840) on the right. The

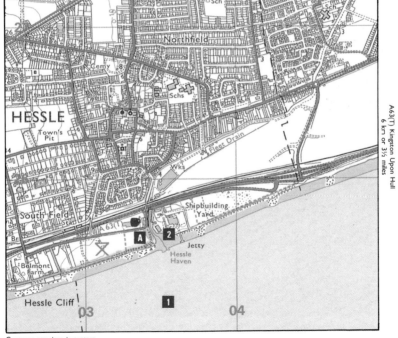

Contours are given in metres
The vertical interval is 5m

*Hessle Haven, a busy Humber shipyard and starting point of the Wolds Way.*

foreshore path from here to North Ferriby can be impassable during severe south-westerly storms. The water traffic and wild-life are the principal, and unpredictable, features of the walk.

A significant number of barges still ply the estuary, carrying bulk loads like timber, quarry materials and fertilisers to and from the smaller wharfs on the Ouse and Trent. Bigger vessels include tankers and car transporters, the latter bound for Goole – a major port of entry for imported vehicles. If you are lucky, you might see a Humber keel, a flat-bottomed craft with a square rig that was for centuries the traditional means of transporting cargoes of coal, grain and other bulk goods on the river. There is still one preserved Humber keel, the *Comrade*. Also, look out for *Amy Howson*, the sole surviving example of a Humber sloop, flat-bottomed but with fore-and-aft rig. Both are operated by the Humber Keel & Sloop Preservation Society. As you follow the shore westward, the most promi-nent feature ahead is the giant chimney of the Capper Pass Smelting Works, which has a twin on the opposite bank at South Ferriby. Capper Pass is scheduled for closure in the 1990s.

This shingle path east of North Ferriby is being re-routed along the new amenity area immediately above the beach. When you reach the foreshore path **C** next to the walled car park at North Ferriby, care should be taken when there is a spring tide, once in every four weeks. The path is liable to flooding under such conditions and the following alternative should be taken until the river bank defences have been reconstructed. Take the road **D** leading at right-angles away from the Humber, cross the railway bridge and turn left **E** on High Street, which becomes Welton Road, before reaching the busy A63. Rejoin the Wolds Way at the top of Long Plantation **F**. If the river bank is clear, however, continue past the car park and houses.

On this shore **5**, in 1937, two brothers spotted some wood protruding from the mud. When they dug deeper they found the remains of three Bronze Age boats, constructed from bevel-led oak planks and moss caulking bound with yew withies.

Where the trees meet the river **G**, find the timber steps up the bank and follow the path into Long Plantation. You emerge on to the main road **F**. It is a dangerous road to cross, so walkers must use the footbridge 550 yards (500 metres) to the left and return to the clearly signposted stile leading into Ter-race Plantation, then begin the very slight incline of your first Wolds hillside.

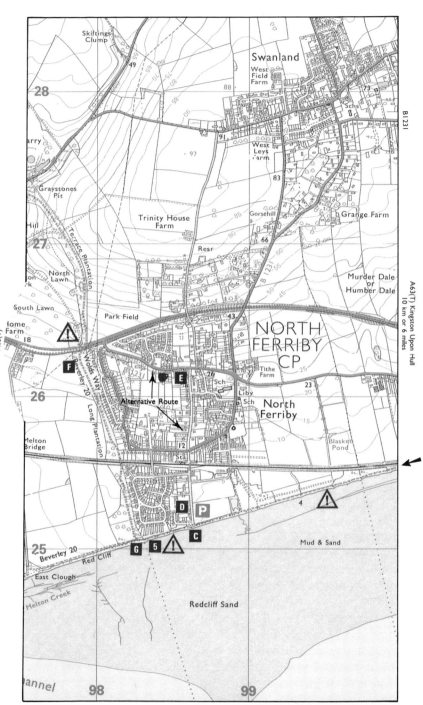

Contours are given in metres
The vertical interval is 5m

39

I km or ½ mile
A63(T) Elloughton

Contours are given in metres
The vertical interval is 5m

Cross the metalled road here and follow the path into Bow Plantation, passing the huge chasm of Melton Bottom Quarry **6**. Turn left on the quarry road **H** and descend to the village of Welton **7** (see page 47), your earliest experience of a Wolds village. It also happens to be one of the prettiest, especially around St Helen's Church and the mill stream.

The Wolds Way continues up Dale Road **I** to one of the most delectable stretches of the entire footpath. Past the modern houses, Welton Lodge and Welton Mill, continue beyond Dale Cottage to the open Welton Dale. This is lined with plantations and is a gorgeous sun-trap in summer. Cross the stile into Welton Wold Plantation and pass a domed mausoleum on the left (there is no public access), built in 1818 by the erstwhile occupants of Welton House, the Raikes family.

Follow the path and waymarks out of the wood, then at the farm road turn left **J** to cross a large field, across which are the impressive Wauldby Manor Farm buildings **8**. Follow the coni-fer plantation (keeping to its east side) for 400 yards (365 metres) until you reach Wauldby Dam, with its mallards and moorhens. Wauldby was once a small hamlet, and there is a little church, obscured by the trees. Turn left then sharp right by the farm cottages and walk on a gently undulating track until you reach a junction, where you turn left **K**. You are accompanied initially by high hawthorn hedges, which are straight for almost 2 miles (3.2 km). This is now classic Wolds terrain, with good views over the patchwork of fields. Follow the signposting along the wide path, past Long Plantation, and you can see a magnificent panorama of flat countryside, west to the industrial towns of West and South Yorkshire.

Join a metalled farm road and descend what becomes Spout Hill, turning right **L** to Brantingham Church when it comes into view. If you wish to visit beautiful Brantingham **9** itself,

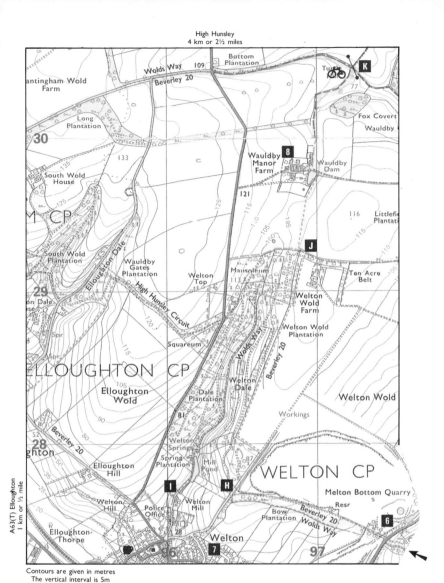

Contours are given in metres
The vertical interval is 5m

continue down the road and turn left into the village. Most impressive is Brantingham Hall, a 2½-storey red brick house overlooking the village pond. Further south is a Gothic war memorial, built from an assortment of features from Hull's Victorian Town Hall (replaced in 1914 by the Guildhall) and described by one expert as 'lovably awful'.

All Saints Brantingham **10**, nestling snugly in its wooded dale, has the most picturesque setting of any church encountered along the Wolds Way, with the possible exception

41

of the ruined St Martin's at Wharram Percy. Bits of it can be dated to the 13th century, but most of what you see today can be attributed to a restoration by G. E. Street, paid for by the wealthy Sykes family of Sledmere.

Continue up the forestry road through Brantingham Dale, a popular destination with motorists from Hull at summer weekends. Cross a stile on the left **M**, which leads on to a gently ascending path, then cross another stile to join a downward track past Woodale Farm **11**. Pass through a gate and continue up to Woodale Plantation. When you reach Mount Airy Farm **12**, turn sharp left at the end of the farmyard, then turn right and descend the curving path to join a county road. It is at this point **N** that those seeking accommodation or refreshments in South Cave should leave the Wolds Way.

## The Humber

Often referred to, erroneously, as the 'River' Humber, this mighty estuary **1** is formed by the confluence of the Rivers Trent and Yorkshire Ouse, which between them drain 9,650 square miles (25,000 square km), equivalent to one-fifth of England's land surface.

The estuary was created more than 70 million years ago when the chalk beds, composed of millions of tiny marine organisms, were thrust to the surface by movement of the earth's crust, and the water – which had once covered them – drained through several massive channels to form new seas. One of the biggest of such channels was the Humber, leaving what became the Lincolnshire Wolds on the south bank and the Yorkshire Wolds on the north. Originally, it drained into the North Sea on the eastern fringe of Hull, but the last Ice Age dumped huge amounts of boulder clay to form what today is known as Holderness, a vast flat area running from Hull to the chalk headland at Flamborough.

It was through the mouth of the Humber that the first settlers arrived from the Continent. Towards the end of the middle Bronze Age period they used simple oak trees hollowed out by fire and crude tools (as evinced by the Brigg boat, found on the Ancholme, which flows into the Humber on the south bank), while late Bronze Age people (890–590 BC) sewed planks together with yew withies (as shown by the discovery of boats **5** at North Ferriby).

Riplingham
3 km or 2 miles

South Cave

Cave Wold

Great Wold
Side

Great Wold
Plantation

Resr

Fox
Covert Farm

**N**

Great Wold

Mount
Airy

**12**

Mount Airy
Farm

The Warren

Woodale
Plantation

Ellerker North
Wold

**M**

Cliffs

Cliffs
Plantation

Woodale Farm

High Hunsley Circuit

Brantingham Dale
Plantation

Rowdales

**11**

93          94          95

Contours are given in metres
The vertical interval is 5m

It was by the Humber that the invaders who were to make the earliest impact on the Wolds, the Parisii, arrived from France around 300 BC. They cultivated the landscape and left traces that can still be seen as earthworks near Huggate and Millington, and a number of chariot burials of their chieftains. Romans and Vikings all used the Humber during their respective invasions; it was the northern frontier of the Roman Empire at one time. Also it was from Immingham Creek, on the south bank, that the earliest Pilgrim Fathers sailed in 1608.

Since the Industrial Revolution, the Humber has been one of the most important shipping lanes in Europe, with navigation schemes connecting the port of Hull with the great inland cities of Sheffield, Nottingham and Leeds and, via the Leeds–Liverpool canal, with the west coast.

Cargo vessels still navigate the gritty brown waters, but the channels and sandbanks are dynamic and have been changing for thousands of years. The shipping lanes have to be regularly altered and river mariners treat the Humber with great respect.

## The Humber Bridge and its setting

The Humber Bridge **3** is arguably the most spectacular man-made structure encountered on any national trail in Britain (historians may prefer Hadrian's Wall on the Pennine Way). End to end, from the cliffs above the Hessle foreshore to the

*Dusk arrives over the Humber Bridge, the world's longest single-span.*

outskirts of Barton-on-Humber on the south bank, it reaches 7,283½ feet or just under 1½ miles (2.2 km) long. Its most important dimension is the single span between the two giant piers: 4,626 feet (1,411 metres), which makes it the world's longest single-span suspension bridge. Toll-paying traffic on dual two-lane carriageways and two pedestrian/cycle paths pass some 150 feet (46 metres) above the estuary. Exceptionally keen walkers can arrive at the start of the Wolds Way via the Viking Way long-distance footpath, which begins at Oakham in Leicestershire and ends 140 miles (225 km) north on the other side of the Humber Bridge.

A regular ferry crossing of the Humber was established in 1825 and operated between Hull Corporation Pier and New Holland until just before the bridge was opened by the Queen on 17th July 1981. Plans for a railway tunnel in the 1870s and a road bridge in the 1930s collapsed through lack of funds, and the present structure, which cost more than £90 million to build and has since run up debts four times that amount in interest charges, is commonly claimed to have been an enticement to electors during a Hull by-election in the 1960s. Its construction was considered essential to the creation of the new county of Humberside (population 850,000) in 1974, formed from the old East Riding and part of North Lincolnshire.

To the immediate west of the north bank pier is the Humber Bridge Country Park 4, a 48-acre (19-hectare) site containing meadows, woodlands, ponds, cliffs, an old mill, nature trails, information centre, café, toilets, etc. The park was formed from an old chalk quarry, first worked in 1317. Access is immediately off the Wolds Way by clearly signposted footpaths leading away from the shore.

## Barton Clay Pits

Extending either side of the Humber Bridge on the south bank are Barton Clay Pits, a 5-mile (8-km) strip of flooded clay workings interspersed with farmland and some industry. The pits are important for both recreation and wildlife. Activities here include sailing, windsurfing and water-skiing, as well as year-round angling. The area has a rich bird life, including bearded tits, which live in the reedbeds. At the western end is Far Ings, an attractive open-access nature reserve run by the Lincolnshire and South Humberside Trust for Nature Conservation.

Clay from this area was used extensively in the local roof pantile industry. Almost directly under the bridge is an area where clay is still being dug for tilemaking, and nearby is a tileworks that still uses the traditional processes. Visits round the tileworks are included in a programme of events and activities within the Clay Pits. Full details of these, and other information about the area, are available from the Information Centre at the Old Boathouse in the Bridge Viewing Area. Tel. Barton-on-Humber (0652) 33283.

## Humber bird life

It is on the first stretch of the Wolds Way that the greatest variety of bird life may be seen. The Humber 1 is recognised as one of the most important bird feeding grounds on the east coast. Wading birds that are present at most times of the year include dunlin, redshank and oystercatcher, joined at the spring and autumn migration periods by large numbers of knot, sanderling, curlew, grey and ringed plover, bar-tailed godwit and perhaps the odd rarity, all of them probing the intertidal mud for bivalve molluscs and polychaete worms. Species of duck include mallard and shelduck, plus the occasional teal and wigeon. In addition, up the estuary some 10,000 pink-footed geese winter annually and some wander downstream. The shore between the bridge and North Ferriby is hunted by short-eared owls and kestrels and there is often a solitary heron for company. The Humber Bridge Country Park 4 beside the bridge is good for the common species of warblers in spring and summer.

## Welton

The village of Welton 7, now an expensive dormitory for Hull commuters, is not only one of the most charming to be found along the Wolds Way but also has perhaps the greatest claim to fame. It was here in 1739 that the legendary highwayman, Dick Turpin, scourge of all coach travellers between London and York, was arrested.

The full story of how he came to be in this seemingly peaceful village can be learned in the Green Dragon Inn, Cowgate, which is as good an excuse to take refreshment as you will ever get. A copy of his record of arrest, to be found inside the pub, says that one John Palmer had stolen some horses in Lincolnshire and driven them across the Humber to sell them. He got drunk at the Green Dragon, shot a gamecock and was subsequently unmasked as the famous Turpin. He was tried at York Assizes and sent to the gallows.

# A CIRCULAR WALK FROM BRANTINGHAM
*6 miles (9.7 km)*

This brief introduction to classic Yorkshire Wolds countryside begins at the duck pond, Brantingham **9**, one of the most picturesque villages in the area. Walk up the hill to the rusting old parish pump, following the Wolds Way and the reassuring 'No Through Road' signs up Spout Hill. Turn right at a clearly marked stile, taking an obvious path through a long, narrow strip of woodland. Keep walking until you reach a forestry track, then turn right, and immediately left on a minor path that goes downhill through the trees and leads into the very pleasant upper reaches of Elloughton Dale. The path joins a minor road, on which you turn left and walk uphill for about 400 yards (365 metres) until you reach a well-signposted path on the right that climbs up steep steps through the wood-land, marked as Wauldby Gates Plantation. This fine aerobic exercise comes to an end quickly and the remainder of this woodland section is on the level or on a gentle slope.

*Wolds Way walking on a crisp winter's day. Brantingham Church lies in the valley below.*

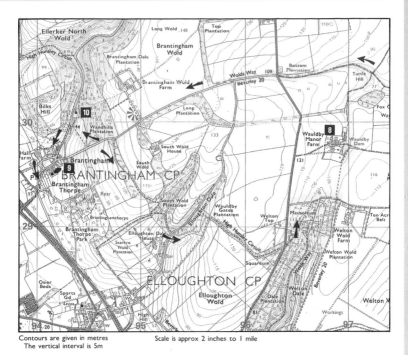

Contours are given in metres
The vertical interval is 5m

Scale is approx 2 inches to 1 mile

When you reach a woodland path crossroads, walk through the woods that spread from across the Wold hillside down into the top end of Welton Dale. The path curves round to the left, and then you turn left on the metalled road, past the riding centre at Welton Top. Turn right on the field path beside the access road to Welton Wold Farm. A domed mausoleum can be seen through the trees on the right (less visible with summer's greenery). This is the tomb of the local Raikes family, built in 1818, but there is no public access. Turn left beside a long plantation of conifers to walk along the Wolds Way for 400 yards (365 metres) to Wauldby Manor Farm **8**, a splendid late-Georgian farmhouse with a chapel built to serve the hamlet of Wauldby. The dam has moorhens, coots and mallards.

Turn left at the top of the pond, then right past the farm cottages along a track that gently undulates to Turtle Hill, and left again for a virtually straight, 2-mile (3.2-km) walk. This takes you along level or sloping tracks, a minor road, and one of the best-preserved green lanes in the Wolds, back towards Brantingham. At the end of Wandhills Plantation on the right, halfway down Spout Hill, take the Wolds Way link path to Brantingham Church **10**, and return to the village by the dale road.

*Brantingham Church, centrepiece of a popular and picturesque dale.*

# 2 South Cave to Goodmanham

*past North Newbald*
*11 miles (17.7 km)*

This stretch of the Wolds Way could easily be accomplished by four hours' solid tramping, but such an exercise would deprive the walker of the chance to explore some of the more interesting features to be found within easy reach of the route. Therefore, by all means permit yourself a late start but leave room for a look around South Cave, some minor off-path walking to such fascinating sights as Newbald's church, and a significant detour for those planning a night's stop at Market Weighton.

South Cave **13** was almost certainly inhabited during Roman times, lying as it did on the main road from Lincoln to York, but there are no surviving relics from this period. Unusually, there are two 'ends' to the village. The West End is centred around All Saints Church, a Victorian restoration of a medieval building, and it was here that the earliest settlement was established. Charters for markets and fairs were granted in 1291 and 1314, but in the Middle Ages the market moved half a mile eastward to what is today's main village centre. The most interesting building is the Market Hall in (what else?) Market Place, a yellow-grey brick structure built in 1796. Up the hill is Cave Castle, a castellated Gothic house built in 1804 for the Barnards, wealthy Hull shipping merchants, but now converted into a hotel.

South Cave is mostly a dormitory for affluent Hull commuters, but it also has good accommodation and a couple of pubs, which make it a handy stop for Wolds Way walkers.

To rejoin the national trail, walk back up the tarmac lane (signposted Riplingham) and just beyond the village find the path **A** leading to the left. This route ascends gently to Little Wold Plantation, where you turn right and walk alongside it for about half a mile (800 metres). This offers splendid views south across the Humber. When the path joins a track, turn right and descend the slope to Comber Dale, going left **B** down into one of the most serene parts of the walk. Just before the point where the path curves right into Weedley Dale is Weedley Springs, from which North Cave's stream rises.

Through the gate ahead is a section of the dismantled Hull–Barnsley railway line **14**, which is followed for nearly half a mile (800 metres) and stops just short of the 2,116-yard (1,934-

metre) Drewton Tunnel (now sealed). Take the steps leading up the steep embankment on the left and follow the path into West Hill Plantation and the lovely East Dale. At the head of the dale, the path arrives at a stile. This marks the end of the path's route across the wooded slopes of the Southern Wolds. From here, the Wolds Way crosses wide expanses of chalk tops and follows deep, mainly grassy, dry valleys.

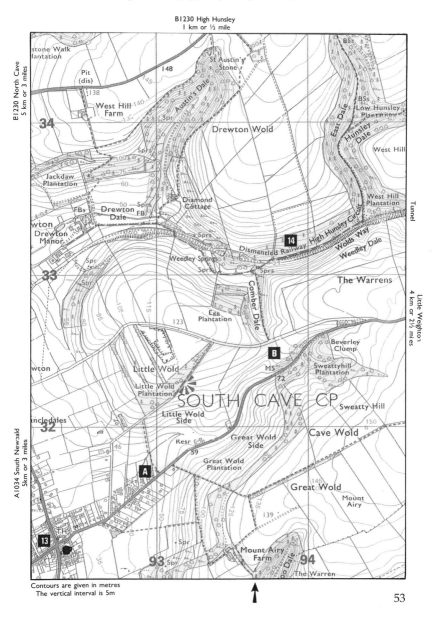

Contours are given in metres
The vertical interval is 5m

*The view east towards Coomber Dale from a green lane.*

Turn left and follow the field edge round to the B1230. Cross the road on to another field path, which twists and turns and crosses another road. The radio mast that you can see is at High Hunsley and transmits BBC programmes to the area. Cross over a stile and descend to the dale, on a barely defined path that is nevertheless easy to follow because it simply keeps to the course of the valley, joining Swin Dale. The dew pond **15** is of the modern type: concrete-lined rather than built on a man-made saucer of mud or clay as was the practice of Anglo-Danish settlers.

Walkers wishing to make a detour to North Newbald should fork left **C** at the end of the dale on a path that joins a metalled road for half a mile and leads into the village.

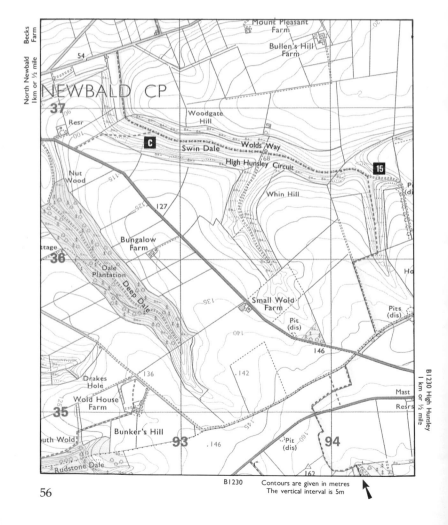

Contours are given in metres
The vertical interval is 5m

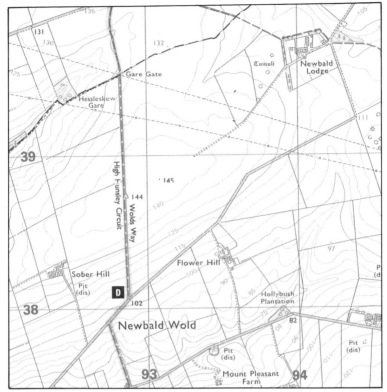

Contours are given in metres
The vertical interval is 5m

The most interesting feature is its famous cruciform St Nicholas Church, said to be the finest Norman church in the East Riding. It was built around 1140 and has been exceptionally well preserved. Newbald also has a classic village green, two good pubs and the timeless atmosphere of an English village, the like of which you will not find further north on this walk. If walking from South Cave, it makes an excellent lunch stop.

The quickest way back to the national trail is to leave the village by the lane that passes the school and Becks Farm, then take the road on the left and rejoin the footpath at a signpost pointing left along the Gare Gate track.

Walkers who did not make the detour to North Newbald should have continued ahead at the top of Swin Dale, turning right on the road, left on a track past a small farm, right on a minor road, and left again **D** on the farm track to Gare Gate. The path stretches in a straight line now for about 2¼ miles

(3.6 km), joining the Sancton–Arras road as it passes Hessle-skew farm **16**. Just before the farm across the field on the right (no public access) is a group of trees marking the spot of what was a Roman amphitheatre.

Although there are few clearly visible reminders – mainly some barrows and tumuli in fields that are inaccessible to the walker – this part of the Wolds was one of the greatest settle-ments of the Parisii, late-Iron Age warriors. A square cemetery containing chariots, horse harnesses, skeletons of ponies, bronze brooches, armlets and beads was found a short dis-tance down the Beverley–Market Weighton road.

Cross the busy A1079 with care, follow the farm road **E** and pass between the buildings at Arras, then pass through a gate and follow a hedge out into open countryside again. This path eventually descends into a valley known as the Market

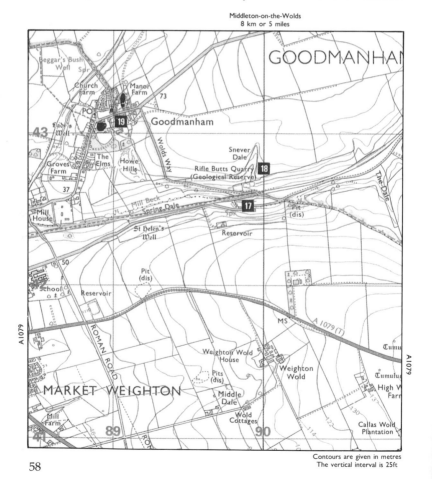

Middleton-on-the-Wolds
8 km or 5 miles

Contours are given in metres
The vertical interval is 25ft

Weighton Gap, through which the North Eastern Railway constructed a line **17** between Beverley and Market Weighton in 1865. This is now a bridleway and footpath known as the Hudson Way, named after the great railway builder, George Hudson.

It is a pleasant spot. Unfortunately, the very interesting Rifle Butts Quarry **18**, a reserve managed by the Yorkshire Wildlife Trust, is not open to the public.

Walkers have a choice to make here: whether to spend the night at Market Weighton or walk on to Goodmanham. Walkers continuing along the Wolds Way to Goodmanham should follow the signposts away from the railway line, northwards on the metalled lane into the village, turning left on to the main village street. The 'finishing post' of this particular section of the national trail is the small village church **19**. Those pausing in Goodmanham (see page 64) for refreshments may wish to walk a short distance farther down the hill from the church (off the Wolds Way) to the Goodmanham Arms (open during normal licensing hours).

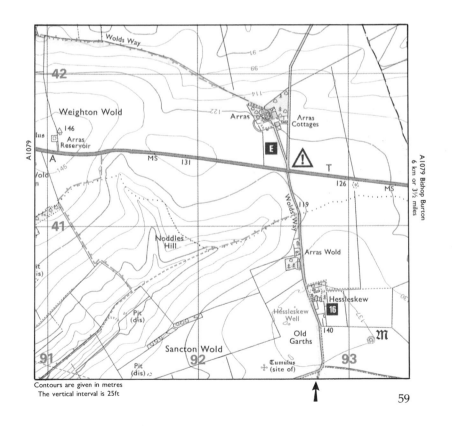

Contours are given in metres
The vertical interval is 25ft

If you are intending to stay in Market Weighton: from the Market Weighton Gap it is an easy walk along the course of the former Beverley–Market Weighton railway line 17 into town. For most of the route, there are high embankments on either side, piled with hawthorn entangled with brambles and nettles. The walker's attention will be diverted by finches, tits and members of the thrush family, in autumn including fieldfare and redwing, which feast off the berries.

As the line reaches the built-up area, another railway joins from the right: it once linked Market Weighton with Driffield. At the end of a development of modern houses F, turn left on the road and you will quickly be in the town's main street 20 (see page 64).

The route back to the Wolds Way is found by walking along the York Road from the centre, crossing a stile G to the right beyond the new housing development, and following a rough path over a field to its left-hand corner. Continue in a straight line through several fields known as Weighton Clay Field, cross the road and pass through Towthorpe Grange farm. Go through the gate and keep to the track which, shortly, joins a road for a brief distance before turning right through the gates of Londesborough Park 21. The Wolds Way is rejoined beyond the lake, just before the track enters a gate at some red-brick pillars.

## Old railway lines

On this stretch of the Wolds Way walkers encounter three disused railway lines, indicating that prior to the cuts of the 1960s the area was well served by connections through to the industrial West Riding.

The Hull–Barnsley Railway 14, followed for a short distance in Weedley Dale, has the most interesting history of the three. It linked Alexandra Dock in Hull with the Yorkshire coalfields and was a direct challenge to a line already operated by the North Eastern Railway. The new line took a workforce of 4,900 men to build and opened for business on 20th July 1885 but, while coal exports via the line soon quadrupled, the competing company lowered its charges and the new line encountered severe financial difficulties. Inevitably, the two merged in 1922. Most of the line is private with no rights of way along it.

The Market Weighton–Beverley line 17 was opened by North Eastern Railway on 1st May 1865, running through a

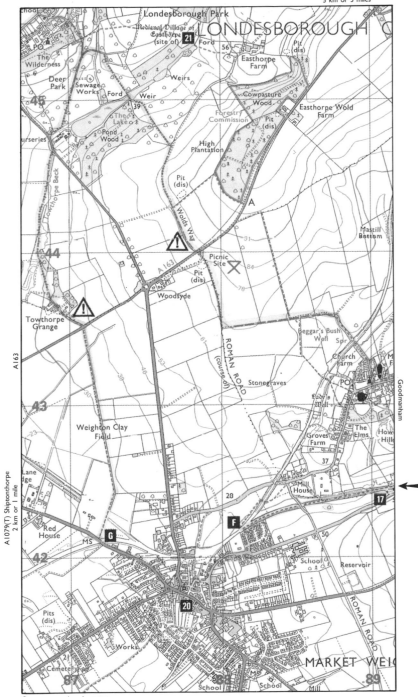

Contours are given in metres
The vertical interval is 25ft

61

*The line in winter: looking along the old Market Weighton–Beverley railway, near Goodmanham.*

natural valley known as the Market Weighton Gap. Its last train ran on 29th November 1965. The line was lifted and today it is a walkers' footpath known as the Hudson Way, named after George Hudson, 'The Railway King' (see page 92), who had fallen from grace by the time of the line's construction. It joins the town with Cherry Burton and will be used by Wolds Way walkers planning a stop at Market Weighton for accommodation. It also forms part of the excellent circular walk from Goodmanham. It is owned and managed by Humberside County Council.

The Market Weighton–Driffield line **24** (see pages 69 and 71) is seen at Goodmanham and Enthorpe. The line's construction was quite recent, opening on 18th April 1890. Originally there were plans to link it with the Hull–Barnsley line but its main traffic was passenger trains carrying West Riding families to the seaside at Bridlington. It was closed in August 1965 and is now in private ownership.

## Oilseed rape

The most dramatic new feature on the landscape of the Yorkshire Wolds is undoubtedly the great yellow sheets of oilseed rape that flare all along the footpath in spring and early summer.

The crop is one of the *Brassica* family, which includes cabbage, swede and mustard, and it originated in the Mediterranean region. It first became a popular English crop in the south in the early 1970s and slowly worked its way north, its popularity increasing roughly at the same rate as concern that high consumption of cholesterol and saturated fats was linked with heart disease.

As the name implies, the crop is grown for its seeds, which do not ripen until late in the season, so it is harvested in August and September. The oil is extracted for use in margarines and cooking oils, and a great deal of the latter is exported from Britain to the Middle and Far East. The remaining vegetable matter is processed for cattle feed.

As demand for unsaturated fat products has grown, so has the number of fields blazing yellow as far as the eye can see from April to July. Wolds farmers have also found that oilseed rape is a useful 'break crop', when grown in soil that has been planted with cereals like wheat and barley for several successive years. This breaks the cycle of infection by diseases that afflict cereals.

There have been two side-effects of this greatly increased production. One is the growth in bee population – the brilliant yellow flowers contain good nectar for the worker-bees to collect. The other is the dramatic rise of the pollen count – the crop is blamed for increased misery for thousands of hay-fever sufferers. Therefore, Wolds Way walkers who have this particular problem should be warned that the pollen count in East Yorkshire can be significantly higher than around towns and cities in other parts of Britain.

## Market Weighton

Once the busiest rail junction in the East Riding, outside Hull, with four lines meeting at its now demolished station, as well as an important crossroads of five main roads, Market Weighton **20** was an extremely busy place until the 1960s. It appeared in *Domesday* as *Wicstun* and received a market charter in 1251, but it was mainly a small village built around All Saints Parish Church, which was begun in the 11th century.

The village became a town as a result of the construction of the Market Weighton Canal in 1772, an 11-mile (18-km) waterway to the Humber on which was carried much of the East Riding's agricultural produce and quarried chalk. It closed in 1900.

John Wesley preached at the Methodist church in Market Place, but perhaps the town's greatest claim to fame, though, was the Yorkshire Giant, William Bradley, who was born here in 1787. He matured to a height of 7 ft 9 in. (2.36 metres), weighed 27 stone (172 kg) and became a celebrated fairground attraction throughout England until his death, due to consumption, at the age of 33. You can see a memorial tablet marking his grave *inside* the parish church – it was feared that grave robbers would steal his remarkable corpse if it had been buried in the churchyard. There is also a tablet on the wall of his birthplace (at the top of Linegate) showing the precise size of Bradley's boot. The doorway of the house was specially constructed to take his great bulk.

## Goodmanham

It is difficult to believe that this sleepy village was the scene of a crucial event in the coming of Christianity to Britain. A heathen temple stood on the site now occupied by the little Norman church when, in AD 626, Edwin, the Saxon King of Northumbria, was converted to the Christian faith by

*In a giant's footstep: William Bradley's amazing boot print on a wall at Market Weighton.*

Paulinus, the great missionary. Edwin, led by his High Priest, Coifi, then set about desecrating the temple. The Venerable Bede described 'Goodmundingaham', as it was then called, as 'this one-time place of idols'.

Nothing of the temple remains today, but the church **19**, in the centre of this spread-out village, is now most notable for its highly decorative 15th century font, perhaps the most outstanding in the Wolds. It stands on a short stem and is 5 feet (1.5 metres) high with rich carving over the bowl's eight sides.

*All Saints Church, Goodmanham, built on a site once occupied by a pagan temple*

# Kiplingcotes Derby

One of the most historic features to be found in the Yorkshire Wolds is the Kiplingcotes Racecourse, home of England's oldest horse race. Although not on the route of the Wolds Way itself, the entire length of the 4-mile (6.4-km) track, covering a rough green lane that has been partly tarmacked on its final section, is included in the excellent circular walk from Goodmanham (see page 69).

The date of the first race, as painted on the winning post **23** (see pages 69 and 70), is 1519, but the earliest actual record of the race was not until 1555. The Kiplingcotes Derby is still run every year on the third Thursday of March, for prize money that is less than £100, being the interest on an endowment provided by 'five noblemen, 19 baronets and 25 gentlemen' in the 17th century.

By horse racing standards, the Derby is a pretty inelegant affair, with spectators apt to end up with a fair spattering of mud. Most competitors are amateur riders, often from the local farming community. The rules state that horses must be able to 'convey horsemen's weight ten stones, exclusive of saddle, to enter at ye post before eleven o'clock on the morning of ye race. The race to be run before two.' The most interesting feature of the Derby is that the person coming second receives more than the winner. He or she gets the entrance money, whereas the victor gets only the interest on the original sum.

# A circular walk from Goodmanham
*13 miles (21 km)*

This excellent route makes a fine introduction to the Yorkshire Wolds, taking in as it does so many of the landscape's classic features, such as the peaceful chalk downs, the quiet Wolds lanes, an unspoilt village, disused railway lines and the historic Kiplingcotes Racecourse.

Begin from Goodmanham Church **19** and walk along the Wolds Way down the hill and all the way to Londesborough village. Pass Warren Dale farm **22** along the back of the village, then leave the Wolds Way by taking the sharp right-hand turn signposted to Nunburnholme and Warter. Pass a gurgling reservoir tank on the right and follow the road for about $1\frac{1}{4}$ miles (1.9 km), then turn right on to the road signposted to Middleton.

Although a large part of this walk is on tarmac, you will not resent it because traffic is virtually non-existent and the views are superb, especially over the Forestry Commission's Rosemary Coombe down to the right. After almost 2 miles (3.2 km), turn right on to the road signposted to Market Weighton. The tarmac is a narrow strip and the grass verges are wide, which indicates the course of an ancient green road. On the left you will see the winning post **23** for the famous Kiplingcotes Derby (see page 68), England's oldest horse race. Straight on at the crossroads with the busy A163 road to Bridlington is the dirt-track section of the race, which continues for three-quarters of a mile (1.2 km) to Enthorpe Wood – a sizeable rookery. The track narrows here and joins a metalled farm road. Go over the bridge at Enthorpe Cutting to cross the disused Market Weighton–Driffield railway line **24**, continue across the county road and after about 1 mile (1.6 km) turn right at the crossroads. At the next T-junction take the track ahead to Kiplingcotes Station **25** on the old Market Weighton–Beverley railway line **17**, now a footpath known as the Hudson Way and owned by Humberside County Council. Although the Hudson Way is a footpath, permissive use by cyclists and horseriders is possible. This path passes the Yorkshire Wildlife Trust reserve at Kiplingcotes Chalk Pit (nearly 20 species of butterflies have been recorded) and joins the signposted Wolds Way, which goes back into Goodmanham.

(for map see pages 70–1)

Scale is approx 2 inches to 1 mile

Contours are given in me
The vertical interval is 2

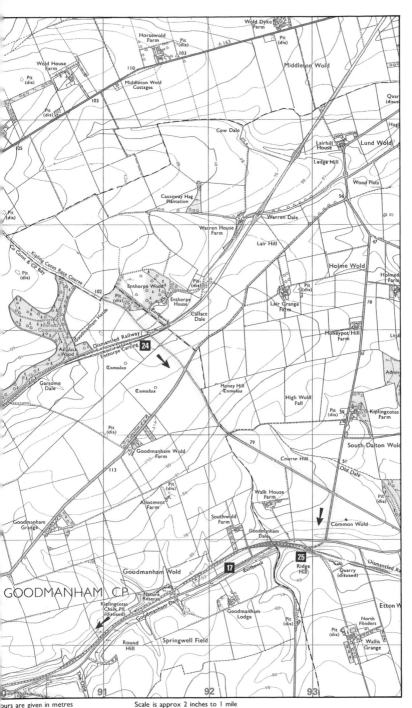

Scale is approx 2 inches to 1 mile

ours are given in metres
vertical interval is 25ft

# 3 Goodmanham to Thixendale

*through Londesborough and Fridaythorpe*
*20 miles (32.2 km)*

This section of the Wolds Way is the longest described here. However, it could easily be broken into two shorter stages. For instance, the overnight stop could be at Millington, a fairly effortless 8-mile (13-km) walk from Goodmanham. This would provide an opportunity to explore the nearby Millington Pasture and Millington Wood (see pages 78 and 93), both of which do not lie on the footpath. Alternatively, the walker could continue to Huggate, a more demanding 13 miles (21 km) from Goodmanham, and find overnight accommodation there. This would permit a shorter walk the following day on the 7-mile (11.2-km) stretch to Thixendale, along some classic dry valleys that certainly repay being savoured at leisure.

The path resumes from Goodmanham Church **19**. Turn right down the hill, past a modern housing development, and join the clear dirt track as it goes under the bridge that once carried the Market Weighton–Driffield railway line. Follow the rutted track straight on, curving round the field edge and keeping a drainage ditch on your left. The path swings round to the right, straightens out and emerges at the top of a very large picnic area beside the main A163 road, which connects the cities of West Yorkshire with the popular seaside resort of Bridlington. There are timber tables and benches at which to enjoy a break, if you wish, but Wolds Way walkers will soon have a choice of infinitely more peaceful picnic sites as the path traverses Londesborough Park **21**.

Turn up the hill slightly, cross the road with care, and join a track – actually part of the Malton to Brough Roman road – through a field, keeping the hedge to your left. The fertile Vale of York spreads out flatly to the west and ahead lie the red roofs of Londesborough. This track links with a metalled road coming up from the left and proceeds forward into the Londesborough Estate. At the landmark circle of six huge horse chestnut trees, fork left **A** over a stile and go down the gentle slope, fording the stream by a plank bridge. The stream issues into the artificially created Londesborough Lake, part of the Park **21** laid out by the third Earl of Burlington in the 17th–18th century. The original Hall was demolished in 1819, its materials used for an addition to Chatsworth, and was

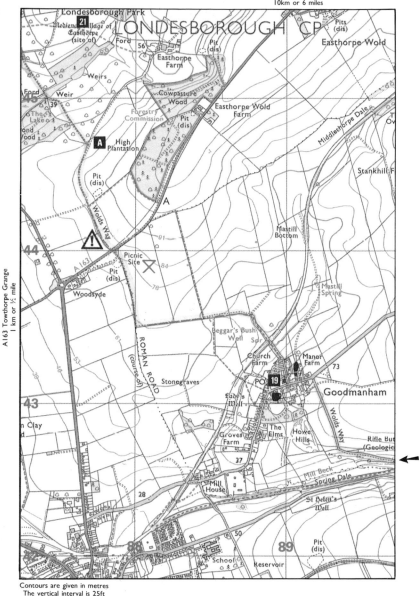

Contours are given in metres
The vertical interval is 25ft

replaced by today's red brick structure, seen in the distance
through the trees. There are, however, some remnants of the
earlier house still visible, notably a stepped terrace, two large
pedestals, some gatepiers and some smaller pedestals dating
from the 17th century.

*Electric sunset: the huge Drax power station, seen in the distance from above*

74

*ondesborough.*

Contours are given in metres
The vertical interval is 25ft

Up the hill, join a track that merges from the left **B**, a section of the Wolds Way for those walkers who chose to stop at Market Weighton. Pass through a gate between the red brick pillars and walk along the track that curves up the hill to the left, through the trees to emerge on a village street in Londesborough. Walkers with the time and inclination to explore the interesting All Saints Church should deviate, briefly, along Low Street to the left. It has a sundial and 11th century Anglo-Danish cross above its Norman south door.

Continuing on the Wolds Way, keep straight ahead up the hill, on a metalled road curving round to the left. Keep straight on again at the crossroads, pass Warren Dale farm **22** and walk along the lane that passes to the north of Londesborough.

Follow the minor road, rarely used by traffic, for just under 1 mile (1.6 km). Turn right at the T-junction **C** and then left through the farmyard of Partridge Hall, leaving it by an orchard and track that skirts Thorns Wood. At the end of the trees you will have a fine view over the village of Nunburn-

76

holme **26**. Cross the stile and proceed ahead, keeping a fence on your right, and follow the field edge round to the bottom corner, crossing Nunburnholme Beck at the footbridge. To reach the village street, go through the small field ahead.

Nunburnholme Post Office (now closed) is a short distance to the right but the Wolds Way turns left towards the church **27**, where the eminent Victorian ornithologist, Francis Orpen Morris (see page 92), was rector from 1854 until 1893. It is worth entering the church to see the fine Anglo-Saxon cross.

Turn right off the road and follow the field edges on to another road. Continue up the slope, and fork right **D** on the track through Bratt Wood. Cross a field, pass Hessey Barn, then go over a stile to another field and a track serving Wold Farm. Do not go through the farmyard but turn left as you reach the farm, join a metalled road, turning right at the house and keeping to the field side as far as the gate. Turn left and go up to the road (linking Pocklington with the village of Warter) and cross over a stile, then follow the path leading to the top of the plantation ahead. Keep the fence on your left as far as the

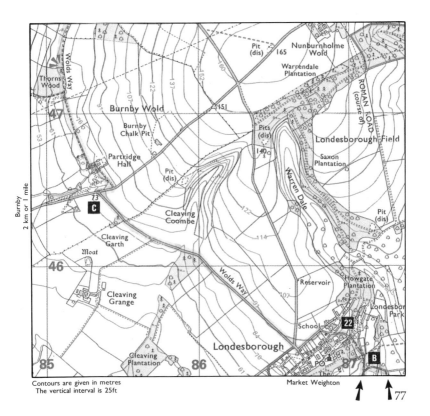

Contours are given in metres
The vertical interval is 25ft

Market Weighton

gate; go through the gate and walk along the track that goes through Low Warrendale Farm and joins a road at a sharp corner **E**. Less than 1 mile (1.6 km) down the road ahead lies the village of Millington **28**.

The Wolds Way now turns right, following the track up the escarpment, to begin one of the most memorable sections. This westernmost ridge of the Wolds is popular with hang-gliders. Behind are fine long-distance views to the south-west. The flat Vale of York floor has three sets of power station cooling towers: Drax on the left, Eggborough in the middle, and Ferrybridge to the right.

As you pass a plantation on the right, the track curves sharp left across the field, then turns down to the left for a short distance, clearly marked between wooden fence posts, and swings right at the point where you are overlooking the village of Millington **28**. From this point, it should be possible to see the tower of York Minster on a clear day.

The next couple of miles (3 km) constitute a magnificent promenade along the ridge overlooking one of the most unspoilt Wolds dales.

Past Warren Farm, cross the dirt track and proceed as before, this time with the hedge on your right. Opposite is Millington Wood, and north of that can be seen the steep sides of Millington Pasture **29** (see page 93).

The path descends via a stile to the well-named Sylvan Dale, with classic chalk banks filled with gorse and grasses untouched by plough or fertiliser. The banks sloping down into Millington Dale at this point are known as Rabbit Warren, a reminder of the once-common practice in the Wolds of 'farming' wild rabbits for their meat and fur. About 30 rabbit warrens were recorded in the Wolds during the 18th century – usually in areas where the land was particularly difficult to cultivate.

When you have just reached the dale floor, the path strikes back up the steep bank ahead, crossing a stile and continuing as before along the field edge. On the left can be seen the line of a substantial linear earthwork **30**, or fortification, which was established by the La Tene tribesmen in the late Iron Age. The double dike would have been constructed to protect their cattle-rearing settlement on these fields.

When the hedge ends, descend the path into Nettle Dale and – there is no way round it – continue straight ahead up the side of the dale. At the top turn right **F** and walk around the

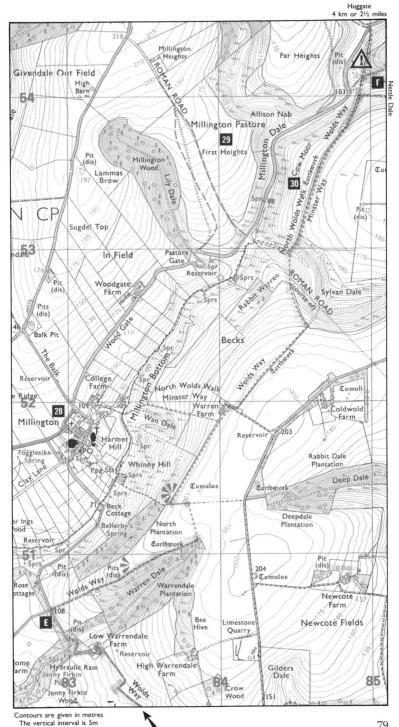

Huggate
4 km or 2½ miles

Givendale Out Field
High Barn
54
Millington Heights
Far Heights
Pit (dis)
103
Nettle Dale

ROMAN ROAD

Millington Pasture
29
First Heights
Allison Nab
Millington Dale
Cow Moor Earthwork
Wolds Way
30
North Wolds Walk
Minster Way

Pit (dis)
197
Lammas Brow
Millington Wood
Lily Dale
Spr
88
Pit (dis)

N CP

Sugdel Top

In Field
Pasture Gate
Reservoir
5pr
Spr
Sylvan Dale
ROMAN ROAD (course of)
185
53
174
Pit (dis)
Woodgate Farm
Wood Gate
Spr
Rabbit Warren

Pits (dis)
46
Balk Pit
Becks
Wolds Way
Earthwork
Tumuli

The Balk
Reservoir
Ridge
52
College Farm
Millington Bottom
Minster Way
North Wolds Walk
Warren Farm
Coldwold Farm

28
109
Spr
Wan Dale
Reservoir
203
Rabbit Dale Plantation
Deep Dale
Millington
Harmer Hill
Spr
Fogglesike Spring
PO
Whinny Hill
Spr
Tumulus
Earthwork
Deepdale Plantation

Clay Lane
Ppg Stn
Sprs
71
Beck Cottage
Bellerby's Spring
North Plantation
Earthwork
Pit (dis)
Tumulus
204

Ings ood
Reservoir
Spr
51
Sprs
Pit (dis)
Pits (dis)
Wolds Way
Warren Dale
Warrendale Plantation
Newcote Farm
157

Rose ottages
108
E
Pit (dis)
Bee Hive
Limestone Quarry
Newcote Fields

ome arm
Hydraulic Ram
Jenny Firkin Pond
83
Jenny Firkin Wood
Low Warrendale Farm
Reservoir
High Warrendale Farm
84
Crow Wood
Gilders Dale
85

Wolds Way

Contours are given in metres
The vertical interval is 5m

79

edge of Jessop's Plantation to a stile. Cross over this and proceed across Huggate Sheepwalk, above Pasture Dale, to a road. Walk along this to the junction, where you follow the signs across the road. The path gradually reaches what is, at around 650 ft (198 metres) above sea level, the highest point on the Wolds Way. From here, when visibility is perfect, it is possible to see as far away as Lincoln Cathedral, the towers of the Humber Bridge and Sheffield in the south, York Minster to the west, and the lighthouse on Flamborough Head to the east.

Cross the metalled lane and follow the path, passing Glebe Farm. On the hillside ahead you can see a diamond-shaped plantation. Larch was planted here to celebrate Queen Victoria's Diamond Jubilee in 1897, but the plantation was felled for mine props during the Second World War and an assortment of trees and bushes grew in their place, preserving the original diamond motif on the hillside.

When you reach the bottom of the track, the Wolds Way turns left but at the junction **G** those who intend to spend the night at the village of Huggate **31**, or who simply wish to use its (limited) facilities, will turn right. At the centre is a large

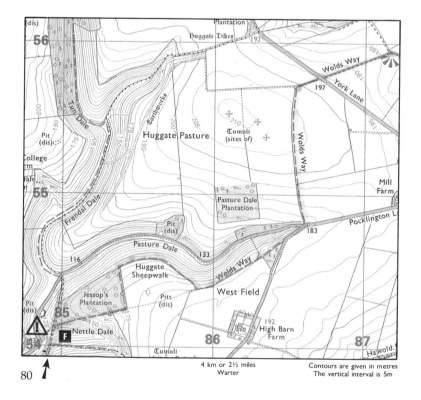

4 km or 2½ miles
Warter

Contours are given in metres
The vertical interval is 5m

village green and a pond on one of the few natural clay basins to have formed above the chalk. St Mary's Church has the locally rare feature of a spire on its 14th century tower. The village is notorious for being cut off for several days at a time after winter snowstorms, since all approach roads involve steep inclines and exposed stretches that suffer from extensive drifting.

If you choose to walk on to Thixendale, follow the track along the sides of some fairly exposed fields, descend gradually into Horse Dale and, at the bottom, curve to the left up the classic chalk valley of Holm Dale. Near the junction of the two dales **32** is the site of one of the many medieval villages wiped out at the time of the Black Death.

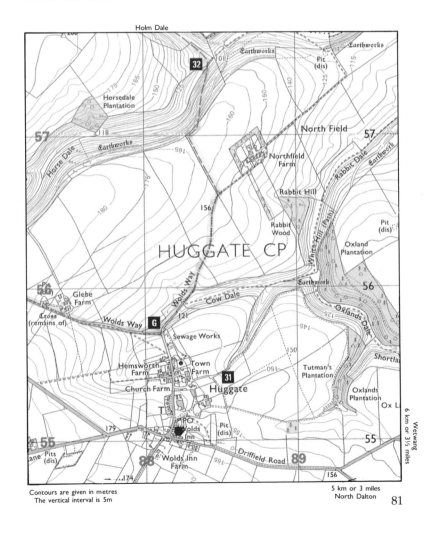

Contours are given in metres
The vertical interval is 5m

5 km or 3 miles
North Dalton

81

*High Wolds in autumn, looking east from near Huggate.*

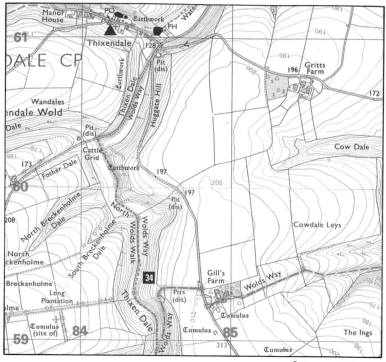

Contours are given in metres
The vertical interval is 5m

The path reaches the dale head and you proceed across a stile below two distinctive horse chestnut trees on a track that emerges on the main street of Fridaythorpe **33**. Turn right and then left on the road signposted to Thixendale. On the left, past the Manor House Restaurant, is a wooden sign commemorating the official opening of the Wolds Way by Lord Middleton, MC, on Saturday, 2nd October 1982. It records that Hessle Haven is 39 miles (63 km) away to the south and that Filey Cliffs are 40 miles (64 km) to the north, making Fridaythorpe the approximate halfway mark.

The village is one of the largest in the Wolds and, as the suffix 'thorpe' suggests, was established by Danish invaders. It is possible that the first half of the name was derived from the Norse goddess of love, Freya. Today's Fridaythorpe is a miscellany of 18th, 19th and 20th century housing. St Mary's Church, behind a farm, is worth seeking out for its south doorway (c. 1120), which Pevsner described as 'utterly barbaric'. It has a jumble of columns, chip-carving, a rope motif, rosettes and decorated scallops.

You complete the final part of this section by walking along a path to the left, opposite Vicarage Farm and beside the edges of four fields before descending steeply, at an angle, into West Dale. Climb up the other side to Ings Plantation, bearing right. The path is difficult to discern on the ground, as it proceeds over a field towards two telegraph poles. However, at Gill's Farm it is easy to see the farm track that joins a metalled lane, on which you turn right. Immediately before a house, turn left on a path that soon curves down into Thixen Dale and the start of one of the most enjoyable parts of the entire Wolds Way.

Follow the line of trees down the chalk valley **34**, pass through a gate, and then walk along a rutted track. Steep, uncultivated banks of grasses and wild flowers rise on either side. Skylarks and yellowhammers are everywhere in spring and summer, as are peacefully grazing lambs and sheep. Swing right on the tarmac lane and left into the main street of Thixendale. The inn is immediately on the right and the youth hostel is a short distance to the left, opposite the post office.

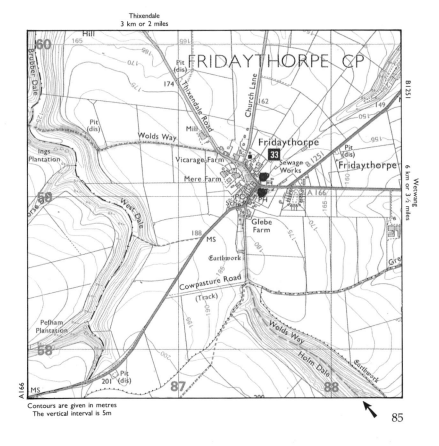

Contours are given in metres
The vertical interval is 5m

*Sheep – once the principal shaper of the Wolds landscape – are seen here in*

## Sheep walks

Until cereal production was increased to feed an accelerating population in the 18th century, the Yorkshire Wolds were covered by sheep 'walks'. The conversion from very early crop-growing to stock-rearing in the Middle Ages contributed to the abandonment of many small villages, as sheep rearing offered greatly reduced employment.

Most of the land seen on the tops today was at one time a vast, grassy sheep walk, but there are still some sections surviving – usually close to the steep banks that ploughs cannot reach. One of the last surviving sheep walks was at Mil-

*Millington Dale.*

lington Pasture **29**, which was finally enclosed for cultivation in the 1960s.

Many of today's field boundaries follow the lines of ring-fences and ditches, used to keep flocks together, and this explains why some fields are positively vast.

## Chalk banks

The plunging banks of the Yorkshire Wolds, seen in places like Millington Dale and at numerous points around Thixendale, form one of the few landscapes in Britain that have been preserved more or less intact for the best part of a thousand years. Woodland clearances from Neolithic times had steadily

*Millington Springs, one of the rare stretches of water in the chalk Wolds.*

created a land suitable for cultivation, but the steep scarps were difficult to manage. The constant cropping of the grasses and seedlings by sheep and rabbits, introduced for their meat and fur, created and maintained the habitat still seen today.

The banks have been preserved and from the calcium-rich soil there springs a highly distinctive flora which, in turn, attracts a wide range of animal life. The major difference is that since the myxomatosis epidemic of the 1950s, which wiped out great numbers of rabbits, natural grazing has been reduced and tall grasses have thrived. There are still many species of wild flowers present in these banks in spring and summer, none more eye-catching from a distance than the cowslip, truly the flower of the Yorkshire Wolds. In some places, its spread actually inhibits the growth of other species. Look out, also, for salad burnet, rock rose, thyme, mouse-ear chickweed, mouse-ear hawkweed, fairy flax, pignut, sheep's fescue, eyebright, burnet saxifrage, harebell and dropwort.

Such a rich flora attracts equally distinctive butterflies, such as peacocks, marbled white, small copper, meadow brown and orange-tips.

## Ponds and streams of the Wolds

Chalk is a highly porous rock and the lack of water supply has been a major factor in the Wolds' colonisation and development. Settlements were mainly situated on the site of springs, such as at Millington and Nunburnholme, but on the high Wolds Anglo-Danish settlers, who established villages like Huggate and Fridaythorpe, created artificial ponds by making an impervious saucer of clay to collect dew and rainwater. You can still see these ponds today as you pass through the villages.

One of the most fascinating features of the Wolds is a natural trough, known as The Great Wold Valley, through which 'flows' the Gypsey Race, an elusive stream. It rises just off the footpath, between Wharram le Street and Duggleby, and flows somewhat erratically south-eastwards to Bridlington. Its name almost certainly comes from 'gypa', which is Norse for a spring. It runs only when the water table in the chalk reservoirs reaches a certain height. Strangely, this is more likely to happen after a dry spell than following prolonged rain. A local superstition has it that when the Gypsey Race runs, famine is imminent. However, it seems to surface every few years but famine – so far – has not occurred.

*A gateway into the Londesborough Estate.*

## Londesborough and 'The Railway King'

The Wolds Way passes through the great Londesborough Estate **21**. Although now said to be a shadow of its former glory, this is one of the most pleasant spots to be found along the footpath. The park itself is thought to have been the site of a Roman settlement called *Delgovita*, and a mansion was built here in the 16th century. Its most celebrated resident was George Hudson, the famous 'Railway King' of the 19th century.

Hudson started out as a draper and eventually went into partnership. In 1827, on the eve of the railway boom, he invested a £30,000 inheritance in railway shares and then helped to gain Parliamentary approval for the York and North Midlands Railway. Three times Lord Mayor of York, he made the city the railway capital of England and bought the Londesborough Estate for £470,000 in 1845 when he was at the height of his success, controlling more than 1,000 miles of railway. He even constructed his own private railway station for the estate, on the York–Market Weighton line, but it has now been demolished. Hudson's reputation was ruined in 1849 when he was accused of fraud in his operation of the Eastern Counties Railway.

## Revd Francis Orpen Morris

Nunburnholme has one great claim to fame. The splendid cream-washed rectory, next to St James Church **27**, was the home of the great Victorian ornithologist, Francis Orpen Morris.

He became rector at Nunburnholme in 1854 when he was in the process of publishing the six-volume *A History of British Birds* and was already busy with a new three-volume work, *A Natural History of the Nests and Eggs of British Birds*. Morris was an acknowledged pioneer of nature conservation in Victorian times and campaigned for bird protection by writing numerous letters to *The Times*; a collection of these letters was published in 1880. He also wrote authoritative books on British moths as well as an encyclopaedic guide to great country houses in Britain and Ireland.

After nearly 40 years at Nunburnholme, Morris died in 1893 at the age of 82. He is buried next to the church door, and in his memory the church bell is inscribed: 'I will imitate your birds by singing.'

## Millington Pasture

The steep-sided valley of Millington Dale has been a popular local beauty spot for decades and the classic chalk banks and tops of Millington Pasture **29** were, until the 1960s, uncultivated downland. Totalling over 400 acres (162 hectares) of close-cropped grass meadow, the Pasture was the last surviving example of the traditional way of open-pasture sheep grazing in the Wolds. It was divided among 108 local farmers, each one awarded a 'gait' or 'gate' comprising pasture for six sheep, or four sheep plus two lambs. (The Gate Inn at Millington, incidentally, was named after this practice.)

Despite a public outcry and mass rambles by local walkers, fences were erected along the narrow road running along the Dale bottom. This ended the hitherto unrestricted access, and some crops were sowed on the higher ground. Nevertheless, the Pasture is still one of the few parts of the Wolds to convey a sense of being in a natural landscape, and it can be enjoyed by walkers taking the circular route from Millington village (see page 94).

Millington Wood, one of the few remaining wooded dales in the Wolds, lies nearby. It is primarily a classic ancient ash woodland and, as such, is a Site of Special Scientific Interest. A path starts from a picnic site and car park and runs right through the woods, enabling you to enjoy a nature walk.

# A CIRCULAR WALK FROM MILLINGTON

*7½ miles (12.1 km)*

This walk combines one of the most memorable stretches of the Wolds Way with exploration of the scenic Millington Pasture and the nearby village. Although it includes much walking on metalled lanes, traffic is usually light and the views offer ample compensation. The entire route should take about three hours, but it can be shortened somewhat at the bottom of Sylvan Dale by returning via the dale road, allowing a visit to Millington Wood (the path into the latter is a cul-de-sac) *en route*.

Begin at the Gate Inn, Millington, walk south along the main street and turn down the hill at Lilac Cottage. Bear right and follow the metalled road up the hill, curving left towards Rose Cottages, then turn sharp left to join the Wolds Way as it follows a dirt track up the hillside. Follow the footpath all the way along the western ridge of the Wolds, overlooking Millington. At the bottom of Nettle Dale, bear left and join the metalled lane to walk back towards the village through the long, dry valley with the steep banks of Millington Pasture **29**. Turn right on a bridle path immediately opposite the pond on a route known locally as Thieves' Sty, part of a Roman road

*Winter sunshine near Millington.*

across the Wolds. Continue over the brow of the hill, joining a track past Millington Heights farm, then turn left on the county road, enjoying the views across the Vale of York to the Pennines. Follow the signpost back to Millington, turning right to look at the church, then left to reach your starting point.

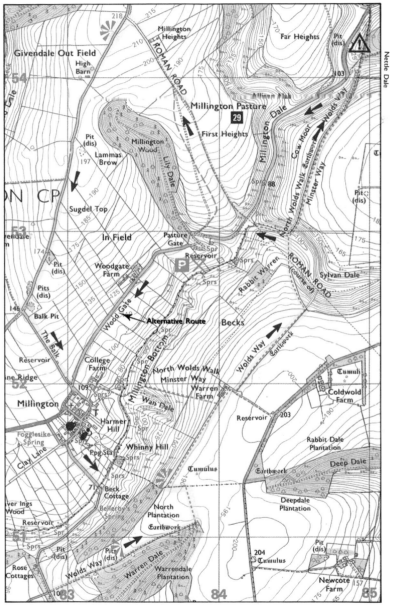

Contours are given in metres
The vertical interval is 5m

*Looking north-west from the Wolds Way above Thixendale.*

# 4 Thixendale to Sherburn

*via Wharram le Street and Wintringham*
*18½ miles (29.8 km)*

This section of the national trail leads through some of the least-frequented countryside in the Wolds – the long northern scarp that rises above Wintringham – but also passes one of the most popular tourist 'honeypots' in the Yorkshire Wolds: the deserted medieval village of Wharram Percy.

There is no more tranquil village in the Yorkshire Wolds than Thixendale. Its mix of traditional and modern dwellings sits peacefully on either side of a single lane that hugs the floor of a straight chalk valley. Contours climb steeply all around, and the serene harmony of birdsong and sheep echoes over the pantile roofs throughout the spring and summer. The only way into the village is by narrow lanes or along footpaths through green dales that have stayed unchanged for centuries.

Six major dales clearly converge here but, with a bit of time studying a large-scale map, it is possible to trace a total of sixteen dales, like the spokes of a wheel, radiating out from the village. This may be the origin of the name 'Thixendale'.

The village has three useful facilities – a youth hostel (the only one in the East Riding), post office/shop and an excellent village pub, the Cross Keys. Thixendale was once served by the church at Wharram Percy but, when that was abandoned, there was no longer a place of worship. St Mary's Church was not built until 1870 and was the work of the Wolds church architect and restorer G. E. Street, paid for by the second Sir Tatton Sykes of Sledmere. He also provided the excellent lych-gate, vicarage and school, the latter now used as a village hall in winter and as a youth hostel in spring and summer.

To continue on the Wolds Way, leave Thixendale at the northern end of the main street **A**, by walking up a track that cuts up the hillside at an angle. Pass Cow Wold Barn on the right, cross the stile and keep to the track as it proceeds along the field edge. The change from the picturesque valley you have just left could not be more dramatic; the terrain here is of open fields, with buildings and hedges at a premium.

Descend briefly into Vessey Pasture Dale and continue up the opposite bank, through a dale offshoot and along the line of an ancient earthwork, turning right **B** on a fine green road that stretches ahead in a straight line for 2 miles (3.2 km). The

*Thixendale, favourite of all villages for many Wolds Way walkers, nestles snugly in its valley.*

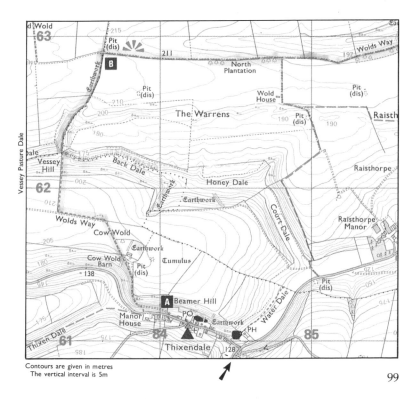

Contours are given in metres
The vertical interval is 5m

fields here are almost prairie-like and it is tempting to assume that modern farming practices have grubbed out hedges to create bigger cereal crops but, in fact, medieval maps show that the field boundaries have not changed for centuries.

At the eastern end of North Plantation, the Wolds Way walker has a choice to make. Either follow the official route or turn left **C** on the public right of way running along the top of Deep Dale and down into one of the most beautiful, peaceful valleys you will come across, in order to see the abandoned settlement of Wharram Percy **35** (see page 108). Those who follow the latter course can rejoin the Wolds Way by taking the track leading east from the ruined village, up the hill to Bella Farm **37**.

If this option is not chosen, continue on the Wolds Way to the top of Tunnel Plantation **36**. Underneath it runs the 1,734-yard (1,585-metre)-long Burdale Tunnel, the longest railway tunnel in the Wolds. It was part of the Malton–Driffield railway line, which was opened in 1853 but closed in 1958. For decades it was the main link to the outside world for many Wolds residents and carried thousands of tons of chalk from the nearby Wharram (also known as Burdale) Quarry, which is now a Yorkshire Wildlife Trust nature reserve famous for its many dingy skipper butterflies.

When you emerge on a tarmac road, follow it left down to Bella Farm **37**, where Wolds Way purists have another chance of deviating left to see Wharram Percy **35** without missing a single step of the footpath. Continuing north, relief from road walking comes at a sharp right-hand bend. Go straight ahead through the field and turn right into the sleepy village of Wharram le Street. St Mary's Church **38** has an Anglo-Saxon nave and west doorway and a Norman tower, but there is little else of interest here.

However, a mile (1.6 km) ahead at the crossroads lies Duggleby, to which the energetic can detour to see the famous Duggleby Howe, a huge round barrow, 20 ft (6 metres) high and 120 ft (37 metres) in diameter, where the remains of 50 late-Neolithic cremations were found, plus an assortment of flint arrowheads, tools carved from boars' and beavers' teeth, and bone pins. It lies 200 yards (185 metres) south of Duggleby Church, just off the B1253.

On the main street of Wharram le Street, turn left and at the end of the village go right **D** on the bridleway that begins up the hillside.

Dogstoop
Plantation

Duggleby

158

Pit
(dis)

Spr

Pits
(dis)

Spr

Home
Farm

**67**

Spr

The Crofts

West End
Farm

Duggleby Dale

Cow Cliff

145

Wand

Broad Balk

140

136

Wolds Way

135

Boyes'
Plantation

**D**

125

Oakhill
Springs

Keeper's
Cottage

Wharram le Street

122

The Ings

122

Red House
Farm

Manor
Farm

128

120

Oak
Hill

**66**

Spr

**38** P.O

140

The Old
Vicarage

150

Spr

146

Station Road

160

Reservoir

Quarry
(disused)

173

Station
House

176

**65**

58

The Ings

Pit
(dis)

Wold
Plantation

Wold Farm

180

WHARRAM CP

Spr

White
Hill

Bella
Farm **37**

**35**

Spr

201

Medieval Village of
Wharram Percy
(site of)

Wolds Way

Bella

Wharram
Percy

Church
(rems of)

Air
Shaft

Alternative Route

Pit
(dis)

B1248

**64**

Drue Dale

Wharram Percy Wold

195

Cumuli
(sites of)

212

208

Burdale Tunnel

195

210

Deep Dale

Air
Shaft **36**

Pit
(dis)

Tumulus

209

Cattle
Grid

Air
Shaft

Fairy
Stones

Fairy Dale

Burdale
Wo

**C**

Earthworks

205

**63**

Wolds Way

North
Plantation

**86**

200

159

Kirk Hill

**87**

Burdale Warren

Contours are given in metres
The vertical interval is 5m

Burdale Quarry

101

*Looking north from a swede crop. In the middle distance rises the famous*

*Neolithic barrow, Duggleby Howe.*

Cross the B1253 and keep straight ahead along the field edge on a track, turning left at a barn and continuing west as the path slopes down to a footbridge across Whitestone Beck. Join the track beyond the oak tree ahead and turn right, following it past Wood House to Settrington Wood. Keep right, following the edge of the plantation. At Wold Barn, the path turns sharp left **E** and swings right to proceed northward again, this time giving views to the west. This is enjoyable walking and the woods are good for spring flowers.

Cross the road into a small plantation that surrounds Beacon Wold, a service reservoir collecting water from a borehole into the chalk. The triangulation pillar on the left is on the 650-ft (198-metre) contour. Proceed through the wood on a path that forms a verdant tunnel in spring and summer as it curves to right and left. When you arrive at a gate, one of the most memorable views on the entire Wolds Way will be revealed. The escarpment tumbles down to Wintringham and the Vale of Pickering is a patchwork of different shades of greens, browns and – when the oilseed rape is in season – yellows. The northern horizon is filled with the lumpy bulk of the North York Moors.

Follow the clear path slanting down the hill and go straight on, reaching a metalled lane **F** that passes Rowgate farm on the

*From Settrington the long-distance views stretch right across to the North York Moors.*

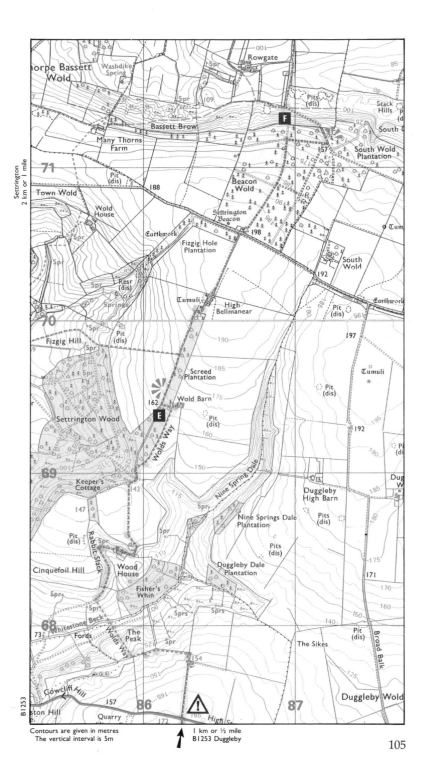

Settrington
2 km or 1 mile

**Thorpe Bassett Wold**

Rowgate

Washdike Spring

001

85

Spr

Bassett Brow

Pits (dis)

Stack Hills

South

F

157

South Wold Plantation

Many Thorns Farm

**71**

Pit (dis)

188

Beacon Wold

Settrington Beacon

Town Wold

Wold House

Earthwork

Fizgig Hole Plantation

198

Tumuli

192

South Wold

Earthwork

Resr (dis)

Spring

Tumuli

High Bellmanear

Pit (dis)

Pit (dis)

197

**70**

190

Fizgig Hill

Pit (dis)

Screed Plantation

185

Tumuli

Pit (dis)

162

Wold Barn

175

E

Settrington Wood

Pit (dis)

160

192

Wolds Way

150

190

Pi (di)

**69**

Keeper's Cottage

142

115

Nine Spring Dale

Duggleby High Barn

185

Dug W

Spr

147

Nine Springs Dale Plantation

Pits (dis)

Pit (dis)

110

Rabbit Stack

Pits (dis)

175

Cinquefoil Hill

Pit (dis)

Spr

Wood House

Fisher's Whin

Duggleby Dale Plantation

171

170

Whitestone Beck

Sprs

Sprs

160

**68**

73

Fords

Wolds Way

The Peak

Spr

140

150

The Sikes

Pit (dis)

Broad Balk

125

Cowcliff Hill

157

154

**86**

Quarry

172

166

High S

**87**

Duggleby Wold

B1253

ston Hill

left. After one mile (1.6 km), turn right at a small reservoir, which collects water from a spring, follow the bridleway along the edges of two fields and cross Wintringham Beck to enter the village.

Turn right on the main street and follow the road round to the left at the gates to Place Newton (a large brick-faced country house dating from 1837), to reach St Peter's Church **39**. This is one of the most interesting churches on the national trail and it is worth pausing to examine what is a rather big church for such a small village as Wintringham. It is constructed from the same seam of Tadcaster limestone that was used to build York Minster and its most fascinating feature is the stained-glass windows of the aisle, each one depicting a 14th

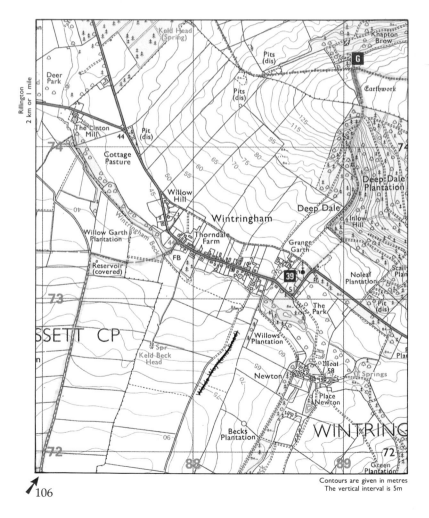

Contours are given in metres
The vertical interval is 5m

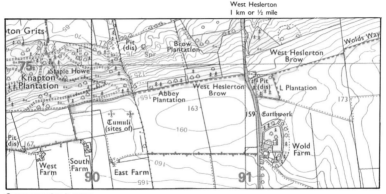

West Heslerton
1 km or ½ mile

Contours are given in metres
The vertical interval is 5m

century saint on a white background stained yellow. Such rich glaziery is considered rare outside York. The wood carving of the pews, pulpit and screens is Jacobean. The church is mainly 14th and 15th century and is remarkably well preserved.

Seek out, also, the following instruction to bellringers provided by Michael Gill, the clerk, in 1723.

> I pray you Gentlemen beware
> And when you ring ye Bells take care;
> For he that Rings and breaks a stay,
> Must pay Sixpence without delay.
> And if you ring in Spurs or Hatt
> You must likewise pay Sixpence for that.

Behind the church, the Wolds Way ascends the hill for about half a mile (800 metres) – crossing a stile and joining a forestry road leading up to the left. Deep Dale Plantation is one of the oldest and most extensive Forestry Commission operations in the Wolds. Parts of it were planted in late-Victorian times.

The steep climb ends at a stile into a field, and you will experience level walking along some ancient earthworks. At a sharp right turn **G**, as the path reaches another plantation, pause to reflect that this also means the end of south–north walking: from now on, the primary direction will be west–east.

Continue past West Farm, and just before South Farm turn down the hill to the left to Knapton Plantation, proceeding eastward again along its edge. This is West Heslerton Brow and at a suitable spot, in clear weather, you may catch your first glimpse of the North Sea. When you reach a lane, make a minor detour round a small plantation masking an old pit and continue to head east with a fence on your left.

107

Turn right **H** to Manor Wold Farm, keeping the trees on your right and joining the farm road briefly. Then turn down to the left and head eastwards again on a path running through fields for more than half a mile (800 metres). Go down the hill, briefly, and follow the sign eastward to Crowsdale Wood. Turn back up the hill a short distance, then walk left along the tarmac road. Walkers intending to spend the night at Sherburn **40** have about one mile (1.6 km) of simple road walking left to do. The Wolds Way continues to Filey by turning right at the first junction.

## *Wharram Percy*

Despite objections from local ramblers, the official route of the Wolds Way bypasses what is by far the most interesting historical feature to be seen along the footpath. Wharram Percy **35** – the best-preserved ruins of a deserted medieval village in England – is well worth a visit. It lies just half a mile (800 metres) off the Wolds Way, near Bella Farm, between Burdale and Wharram le Street. If walking from Thixendale to Sherburn in one day, allow an hour for a detour to explore it.

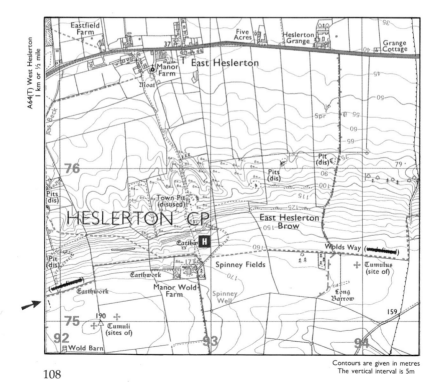

Contours are given in metres
The vertical interval is 5m

Wharram Percy (the name is derived from the old Scandinavian *hwerhamm*, which means 'at the bends', and from the Percies who were lords of the manor in the 12th–14th centuries) was built in the beautifully tranquil Deep Dale. There is evidence of at least one Iron Age house (*c.* 100 BC) having existed here, as well as a Roman farm or villa, but the village grew under Anglo-Saxon settlers. For three centuries it was a compact farming village, with 30 households, a population of 150, a church and a cemetery. However, by the mid-14th century, a combination of the Black Death and a change from corn-growing to sheep-rearing saw its population cut by half. The last house was deserted around the year 1500.

Today, the village is mainly a collection of bumpy earthworks. St Martin's Church contains much of its original 12th century materials and is the most visible relic of Wharram Percy. Most of the village was on the hillside to the west and north of the church and it is possible to make out the grassed-over foundations of peasant houses, a manor house and mill. There is also a reconstructed pond. The site is maintained by English Heritage.

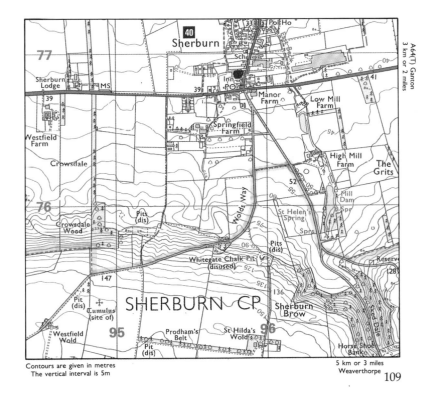

Contours are given in metres
The vertical interval is 5m

5 km or 3 miles
Weaverthorpe

*St Martin's Church in the deserted medieval village of Wharram Percy.*

# A CIRCULAR WALK FROM THIXENDALE

*8¼ miles (13.7 km)*

A tranquil village, unfrequented chalk valleys, sweet hillside pastures and one of the most picturesque Norman churches in the Wolds make this walk a consummate delight, especially on a fine day. Begin at Thixendale Youth Hostel, and walk north to pass through a gate on the left past the tennis courts. Follow the dry valley as it curves round to the left, then branch right up Milham Dale, joining a farm road at the top of the Dale and following this road to the west. Turn left when you reach a metalled road – an old Roman road – and follow this. After a short distance turn right, keep beside the field edge to a stile, and follow the arrows over a succession of stiles, past Woodley Farm, then turn left through a gate at the bottom of the field on to a track. Go up the hill for a short distance until you reach a metalled road, then follow the signpost on the right over fields, and through gates and stiles, on an indistinct path that eventually crosses a bridge over a brook into the graveyard of All Saints' Church **41**, Kirby Underdale. Pause to look round

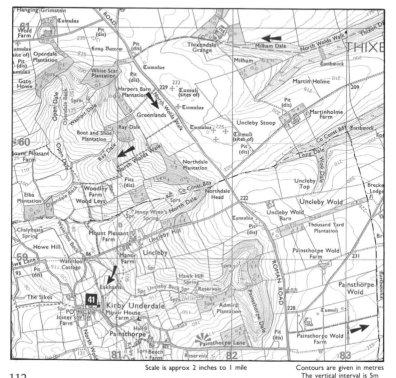

Scale is approx 2 inches to 1 mile

Contours are given in metres
The vertical interval is 5m

the church, erected in the 12th century. Note the herringbone work on the west door. Walkers can explore the church with the use of an excellent pamphlet, purchased inside (put a fee in the honesty box).

Continuing the walk from the church, follow the lane a short distance, take a signposted path on the right through a field to the trees ahead, cross the stile and follow a farm track up to the left. This joins a metalled road, which climbs for three-quarters of a mile (1.2 km), and offers splendid views. Turn left at the top, then right on the straight farm road, swinging sharp left and sharp right where the path leaves the road. Follow the field edge, then go through a gate to a path that leads to the bottom of Worm Dale. This path eventually joins the Wolds Way, which comes down the opposite grassy bank from Fridaythorpe. Turn left to join the national trail and from here it is a pleasant, flat walk back to the village through Thixen Dale.

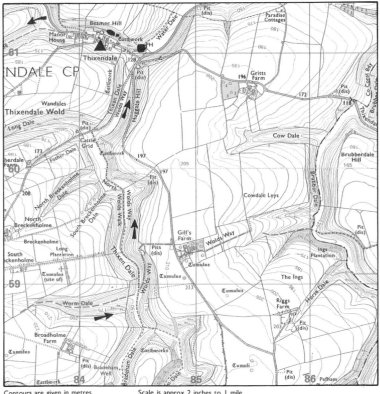

Contours are given in metres    Scale is approx 2 inches to 1 mile
The vertical interval is 5m

# 5 Sherburn to Filey

*through Muston*
*17¼ miles (27.8 km)*

It may be tempting at first to put your head down on this final section and quickly reach the finishing post of the national trail, followed perhaps by a hot bath and a celebratory drink. But then you will walk down Stocking Dale and, suddenly, feel pangs of regret that these fabulous chalk valleys are being left behind for good, and on the grand finale at Filey Cliffs there are few walkers who would not wish to savour the views of some of the finest coastal scenery in England. So by all means get your skates on through some of the more unexceptional field paths; it will allow time to appreciate the finer sections of the walk later on.

Sherburn is shot through by busy traffic heading to and from the coast, and the main place of interest is St Hilda's Church, which contains 11 Saxon stone sculptures.

Leave the village south from the main street, and rejoin the route either by going back up the right fork at Manor Farm and taking the left turning through a field, or by cheating on a few steps of the Wolds Way and forking left at the farm to join the

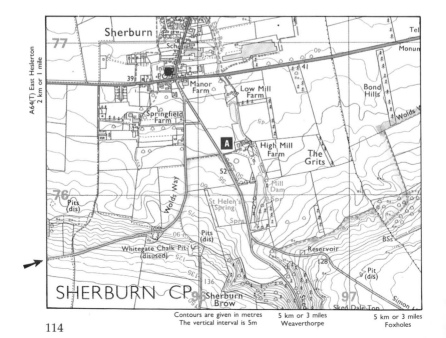

Way **A** on the tarmac lane leading to Butterwick, Foxholes and Weaverthorpe. High Mill, passed on the left, was a fine water-powered mill until well into this century but is now operated by electricity.

Fork left for Foxholes, cross a stile and walk along a field beside a high hedgerow, curving up to a gate into a small wood. Just when you think you are set for a pleasant wood-land walk, the path turns infuriatingly back out into a field, and – to add insult to injury – proceeds *down* the hill.

Swing right on a track, past Manor Farm and Dawnay Lodge, go through two fields, then join a lane and turn right and immediately left. Down the hill is the village of Ganton **42**, with whitewashed houses and a stream gurgling through the main street. It is the most picturesque village in the locality and famous for its international golf course. Ganton Hall **43**, which is glimpsed through the trees farther up the hill, is Victorian and is often likened to a French château.

Turn right, passing stables on the left and the magnificent 14th century spire of St Nicholas Church **44**. Keep to the top of the field until you reach a narrow plantation, then turn right on its east side and follow the path up the hill and over a field,

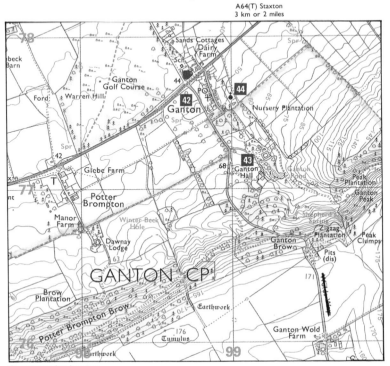

Contours are given in metres
The vertical interval is 5m

*A distinctive Wolds Way signpost near Staxton Wold.*

zigzagging along field edges to the main road. A short distance down the hill is a popular picnic site with superb views.

Cross over and take the road past Grange Farm, refusing to be intimidated by the 'Private' signs for RAF Staxton Wold **45**. The road proceeds ahead for a little under 1 mile (1.6 km) and then turns sharp right at the high fences surrounding the offices and car parks. Follow the road as it goes down a hill past a farm. Where it becomes level, look left for a path going up a slope **B**. Cross the stile and begin a long trek of 1½ miles (2·4 km) along field borders in an almost straight line.

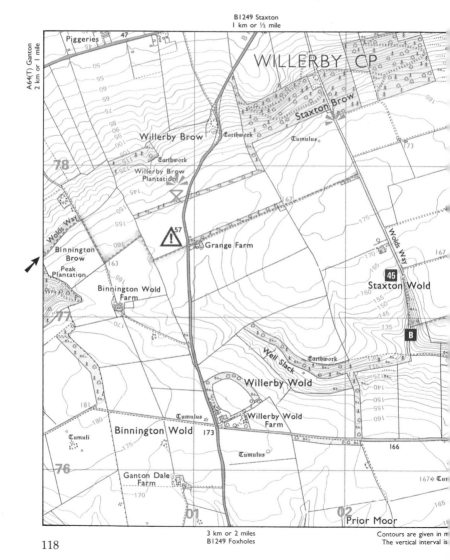

The path emerges on a metalled lane, on which you turn right **C** for 350 yards (320 metres) and then left, walking alongside a fence across the top of Raven Dale. Drop down to Camp Dale and keep following the fence right along the edge of Camp Dale.

Why, you might ask, does the path not simply follow the floor of these lovely dales? The answer may be staring you in the face: bulls run in these fields and footpaths specially created for the Wolds Way national trail were drawn along the safer dale tops.

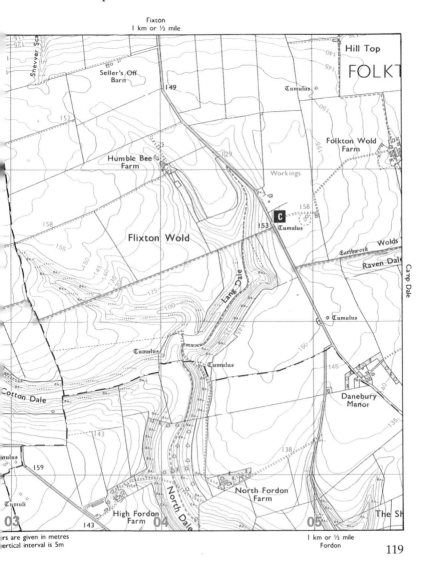

Fixton
1 km or ½ mile

rs are given in metres
ertical interval is 5m

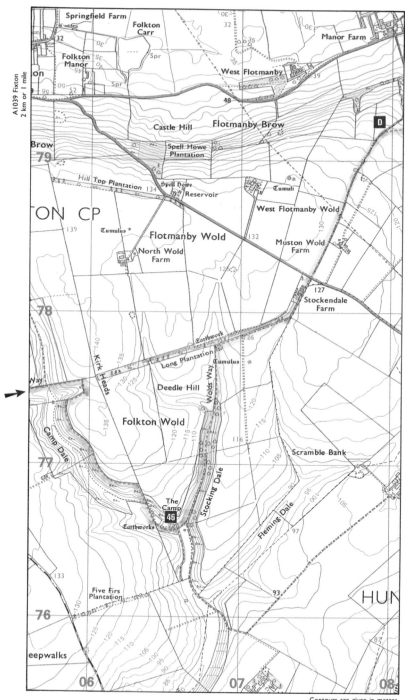

Springfield Farm
Folkton Carr
Folkton Manor
Manor Farm
West Flotmanby
Castle Hill
Flotmanby Brow
Spell Howe Plantation
Brow
79
Hill Top Plantation
Spell Howe
Reservoir
Cumuli
West Flotmanby Wold
TON CP
Tumulus *
Flotmanby Wold
North Wold Farm
Muston Wold Farm
78
Stockendale Farm
Earthwork
Long Plantation
Tumulus
Deedle Hill
Wolds Way
Folkton Wold
Kirk Heads
Way
Scramble Bank
77
Camp Dale
The Camp
46
Stocking Dale
Earthworks
Fleming Dale
133
Five Firs Plantation
93
HUN
76
eepwalks
06
07
08
D
A1039 Fixton
2 km or 1 mile

Contours are given in metres
The vertical interval is 5m

Contours are given in metres
The vertical interval is 5m

Hunmanby

The path eventually reaches the bottom of Camp Dale and turns left into Stocking Dale, your last half-mile (800 metres) of Wolds chalk valley. At the junction between the two dales is the site of a deserted medieval village **46** (marked on Ordnance Survey maps as 'The Camp') but there is little more to see than a few grassed-over bumps.

Follow Stocking Dale into the wood at the top, climbing a slope to a track leading to Stockendale Farm. Cross the metalled road and join a field track that runs for just under three-quarters of a mile (1.2 km) to a stile on the right **D**. This leads on to an indistinct path across a field (rather than following the edge) to a stile in the hedge on the other side.

The field path from here descends the chalk scarp, then leaves it behind as you reach the clay soils of Muston **47**. At the main street, turn right and pass the pleasant old and new houses, many of them holiday 'lets', then follow the road round to a terrace of houses that faces you. The path goes down the right side **E**, crosses two fields and the main A165

Scarborough–Bridlington road, and proceeds through Thorn Balk towards Filey (see page 124). Swing right **F** at the built-up area on a path that joins the main road. Turn left for Filey town centre. Walkers with overnight accommodation already booked in the resort may wish to leave their rucksacks there in order to enjoy the final section light of load.

There are several ways of reaching the Coble Landing **48**, starting point for the walk out to Filey Brigg, but if you wish to follow every step of the Wolds Way, the recommended route is as follows. From the main street, turn right at the Methodist Church along Union Street, right into Mitford Street and immediately left through Reynolds Street to Queen Street, following the path and steps from its seaward end to Coble Landing.

Leave the Coble Landing by a dirt path **G** that leads up the cliffside behind the Lifeboat Station, passing a Wolds Way sign

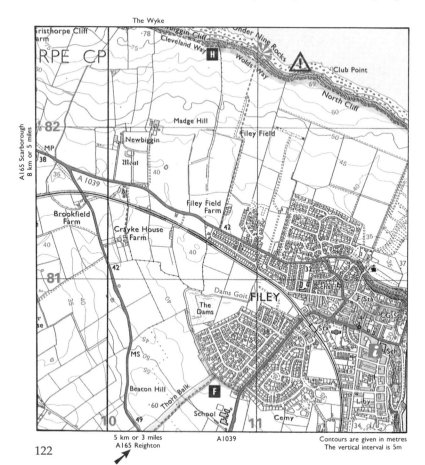

at the bottom, which records the distance from the Humber Bridge to Filey Brigg as 79 miles (127 km). Follow the path along Pampletine Cliffs 49, dropping down a small ravine known as Arndale, which gives access to the clubhouse of Filey Yachting Club. Climb the steps up the other side and follow the cliff edge (with care) past North Cliff Country Park 50.

As you walk out to Filey Brigg 51 (see page 124), there are magnificent views across the bay to the 400-ft (122-metre)-high chalk walls of Bempton Cliffs and Flamborough Head. The former is a Royal Society for the Protection of Birds reserve containing England's only mainland gannetry and nesting site for thousands of razorbills, guillemots and puffins

Walkers who wish to explore Filey Brigg should take the clear path cut into steps down the clay cliff. Return by the same path to the clifftop for the last mile of the Wolds Way, heeding the red and white signs warning of the dangerous cliffs. The path is very narrow in places, as you head north, keeping a wooden fence to your left. The fence ends and the path becomes narrow, between a built-up cliff edge and the side of a field.

The national trail ends at a fence with a stile **H** (formerly the northern boundary of the old East Riding), with dramatic views ahead of the great cliff known as The Wyke, and Scarborough and Ravenscar in the distance. This is also the end of the Cleveland Way.

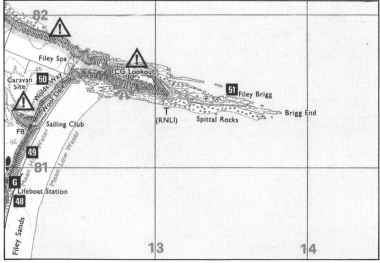

Contours are given in metres
The vertical interval is 5m

## Filey

For many, Filey is the most attractive spot on the Yorkshire coast: a seaside town delightfully free of the worst excesses of holiday resorts, a magnificent bay well sheltered for bathing, windsurfing and yachting, with dramatic views of the chalk headland at Flamborough and Bempton in one direction and the great black finger of Filey Brigg in the other. Add the atmosphere of a traditional Yorkshire fishing village and its unique 'coble' boats, and you have an interesting place.

Filey grew as a fishing community well before the Norman Conquest, and the fishing craft seen at the Coble Landing, flat-bottomed for beach-launching, have their roots in the Viking longboats that were a common sight on this coast more than a thousand years ago. They are used for line fishing for white fish such as cod, haddock and plaice, and for the laying of 'fleets' of crab and lobster pots along the rocky shore.

The Georgian-style houses in the Crescent, overlooking the bay, were built in 1840 when Filey enjoyed brief prosperity as a spa town using mineral waters tapped on the cliffs above the Brigg. The most interesting part of town is in the Queen Street area, still the heart of the fishing community. There is a Folk Museum, and look for the old house at the end of the street, close to the cliff edge, that was once called T'awd Ship Inn and was the haunt of smugglers.

## Filey Brigg

There is no geological curiosity on the English coast quite like Filey Brigg **51**. At low tide the jagged reef, a ¾-mile (1.2-km) protrusion forming an almost perfect right-angle to the bay, has the appearance of an aborted attempt at building a causeway across the North Sea. Thousands of years ago, a huge layer of clay was deposited on this coast by the action of glaciers, but it quickly eroded to expose a solid floor of lower calcareous gritstone that Scandinavian settlers named *bryggja*, meaning landing place.

It may look like a natural jetty on a calm summer's day, but the Brigg is carefully avoided by all craft, big and small, at any time of year. The coastal currents are fierce, onshore winds can be strong and many vessels have been shipwrecked on its black teeth. Anglers have also been swept away by the ferocious breakers. When the seas are high and visibility is poor it must be considered out of bounds, and walkers should always

*Journey's End: the cliffs north of Filey Brigg, with Scarborough in the distance.*

take care on the cliff in mist, high winds and, most important of all, at high tide.

The Brigg is very popular with bird-watchers, who see many rarities making landfall during the autumn and spring migration periods. Winter visitors that are frequently seen offshore include long-tailed ducks, red-throated divers and red-necked grebes. In the summer there are many gannets, kittiwakes and auks to be seen fishing nearby, as well as common and arctic terns. The wooden shack at the foot of the cliffs – once a tea and snack bar – is now a hide for watching seabirds, belonging to the Filey Brigg Ornithological Group, who will rent out a key (ask at Filey TIC, see page 136). Filey Brigg is a twitcher's paradise!

The cliff above the Brigg, known as Carr Nase **53**, was the site of a Roman signal station, one of a series that stretched from Flamborough in the south to Scarborough, Ravenscar and beyond to the north. They performed an 'early warning' function, watching for a Viking invasion and preparing to relay the warning by a series of beacons to *Eboracum*, the great Roman city that is now York.

# A CIRCULAR WALK FROM FILEY

*4 miles (6.4 km)*

This two-hour walk can either be used as a way of investigating Filey Brigg **51** without retracing your steps back along the shore or – in reverse from the end of the Wolds Way into Filey – as an alternative return route into town after completing the footpath. Leave Coble Landing **48** by Church Ravine. Just before the bridge, on the left, notice the old well **52** once used by visiting foreign fishing fleets for their fresh water (it is now considered undrinkable!)

Do not follow the road round to the left but keep straight ahead, towards some new houses, and turn left on Church Cliff Drive, at the entrance to North Cliff Country Park **50**. At the very last house on the right, a gated footpath goes down past Filey Field farm, keeping straight on the track as it follows a hedge, up a gently sloping field, with a ditch on the left. The path eventually reaches the final stretch of the Wolds Way. If

*Filey's flat-bottomed 'coble' fishing craft are descendants of the Viking longboats and are used for line fishing.*

Contours are given in metres
The vertical interval is 5m

Scale is approx 2 inches to 1 mile

you wish to visit the end of the Wolds Way **H** – and the beginning of the Cleveland Way, turn left and walk just a short distance to the north. There are extensive views up the coast to Scarborough and Ravenscar. Turn south on the narrow clifftop footpath to Filey Brigg **51**. Below, on cliffs known as Under Nine Rocks, nest fulmars, kittiwakes, herring gulls and cormorants in season. Cross the springy turf of Carr Nase **53**, and visit the Brigg by the distinct path, avoiding the edge of the dangerous cliffs. The view across the bay is of Bempton Cliffs and Flamborough Head. If weather and tidal conditions allow, drop down on to the Brigg. At low tide only, it is possible to return to Coble Landing **48** on the rocky shore and beach. Otherwise, ascend to Carr Nase **53** once more and follow the Wolds Way in reverse back via the edge of North Cliff Country Park **50** and Pampletine Cliffs **49** to Filey. At the path leading to Filey Yachting Club, you may choose to walk along the beach back to Coble Landing and the start of the route.

*The dramatic clay cliffs and long, rocky finger of Filey Brigg.*

# PART THREE

# USEFUL
# INFORMATION

# Transport

In common with most rural areas, public transport in the Yorkshire Wolds is somewhat sparse. A number of bus services are operated, mainly by the East Yorkshire Motor Services in the Humberside sections and by the Scarborough & District company over the North Yorkshire border, but many of the services are infrequent and of little use to walkers on the Wolds Way. Trains run between Hull and Filey and are most likely to be used at the beginning and end of the continuous walk.

## Rail

Hull is reached by train via Doncaster from the south, York from the north, and Leeds from the west. An East Coast line runs between Hull and Scarborough but crosses the Wolds Way only at Filey. If you walk south to north (as the route is described in this book), you can use the train (frequent all the year round) to return from Filey to Hull. Regular trains also run from Scarborough (two stops north from Filey) to Malton and York, where you join the main BR network. The following telephone numbers are BR information services for times of trains, fares, etc:

Hull (0482) 26033
Driffield (0377) 43148
Bridlington (0262) 67056

Filey (0723) 513166
Scarborough (0723) 373486
York (0904) 642155

## Buses

Timetables for the principal bus services in the Yorkshire Wolds can be obtained from the following operators:

East Yorkshire Motor Services, Hull, 252 Anlaby Road, Hull, HU3 2RS. Tel. Hull (0482) 27142.

Ben Johnson's Coaches, Bowser Lane, Brandesburton, Nr Driffield, East Yorks. Tel. Hornsea (0964) 542475.

Scarborough & District Motor Services Ltd, Valley Bridge Bus Station, Scarborough, YO11 2PD. Tel Scarborough (0723) 375463.

Yorkshire Coastliner, Railway St, Malton, North Yorks. Tel. Malton (0653) 692556.

# Accommodation

At the Humber and coastal ends of the Wolds Way accommodation is plentiful but it is less so deep in the Yorkshire Wolds. The five sections of the footpath as described in this book make the best use of the bed and breakfast/meal facilities on offer, but there are a number of other off-route places at which it is possible to spend the night, and you may wish to lengthen or shorten your day's walking accordingly.

The following is a list of towns and villages where bed and breakfast accommodation may be on offer. Some establishments are seasonal; others come and go according to ownership of the property. Most will do an evening meal, if booked in advance. General accommodation lists for the area giving names, telephone numbers, prices and lists of facilities can be obtained from tourist information centres (see page 136). A short Wolds Way accommodation list is also produced by Humberside County Council Technical Services Department (see address on page 140).

*Accommodation places*

| | | |
|---|---|---|
| Hull | West Heslerton | Huggate |
| North Ferriby | Ganton | Thixendale |
| Brantingham | Muston | Wintringham |
| Newbald | Hessle | Sherburn |
| Market Weighton | Welton | Flixton |
| Millington | South Cave | Filey |
| Fridaythorpe | Goodmanham | Scarborough |
| Settrington | Nunburnholme | |

**Youth hostels**

Youth hostels provide budget dormitory accommodation for people of all ages. They have basic catering/cooking facilities, but there are few of them in the Wolds. The following are the two most likely to be of use to Wolds Way walkers, but it is essential to telephone in advance of arrival.

Thixendale Youth Hostel, Village Hall, Thixendale, Malton, North Yorks, YO17 9TG. Tel. Driffield (0377) 88238. (The warden is also the sub-postmistress.) The youth hostel also has a camp site.

Scarborough Youth Hostel, Burniston Road, Scarborough, North Yorks, YO13 0DA. Tel. Scarborough (0723) 361176.

*Windswept tops at Wauldby, above the southern slopes of the Wolds.*

## Camping

In view of the fact that virtually every step of the Wolds Way is on agricultural land, official camp sites are few and *ad hoc* pitches, of the sort one finds on wilder paths like the Pennine Way, are non-existent. For official sites, contact the tourist information centres listed on page 136. Some farmers allow camping on their land by responsible people and it is worthwhile using the Ordnance Survey maps to pinpoint farms near to your planned overnight stops and writing to the farmer asking for permission or, if he does not allow camping, for advice on whether his neighbours do (do not forget the s.a.e.). The facilities may be basic but a water supply should be available. Never camp anywhere without seeking permission.

## Tourist information centres

Tourist information centres (TICs), run by local councils in the area of the Yorkshire Wolds and beyond, are the best sources of information when you are planning your walk and need advice on such things as accommodation, camping, public transport, local services and places of interest. On the Wolds Way itself there are two TICs – near the beginning, at the Humber Bridge, and near the end, at Filey. Others cover wide areas of the countryside through which the footpath passes. The following list also includes Beverley, Bridlington, Hull, Malton and Scarborough, in case you arrive at them by public transport or wish to explore their immediate areas.

Beverley TIC, The Guildhall, Register Square, Beverley, Humberside, HU17 9AU. Tel. Hull (0482) 867430. Open all year.

Bridlington TIC, Prince Street, Bridlington, Humberside, YO15 2NP. Tel. Bridlington (0262) 673474/679626. Open all year.

Filey TIC, John Street, Filey, North Yorks, YO14 9DW. Tel. Scarborough (0723) 512204. Open Easter; May–September.

Hull TIC, 75/76 Carr Lane, Hull, Humberside, HU1 3RD. Tel. Hull (0482) 223559. Open all year.

Humber Bridge TIC, Humber Bridge North Bank Viewing Area, Ferriby Road, Hessle, Humberside, HU15 0LN. Tel. Hull (0482) 640852. Open all year.

Malton TIC, Old Town Hall, Market Place, Malton, North Yorks, YO17 0LT. Tel. Malton (0653) 600048. Open April–Nov.

Scarborough TIC, St Nicholas Cliff, Scarborough, North Yorks, YO11 2EP. Tel. Scarborough (0273) 373333. Open all year.

## Local facilities

Many Wolds villages are classic examples of settlements where rural services have steadily declined. Useful facilities do exist but they are not numerous. Most pubs do meals or snacks at lunchtime and in the early evening. Some villages have just one bus service per week and these are not included in this list.

Fuller details of amenities can be obtained where there is a tourist information centre (TIC), through a personal visit, letter or telephone call (see addresses on page 136). Further facilities are marked on the maps. Rural services are constantly under review and some may be withdrawn while others, from time to time, might be added. Some of the village post offices have limited opening times. Along the footpath, it is always worth asking a farmer or fellow-walker the whereabouts of a facility that you require.

Hull: all facilities
Hessle: all facilities (TIC at Humber Bridge viewing area)
North Ferriby: bus, café, PO, pub, shop, tel, wc
Welton: bus, PO, pub, shop, tel
Brantingham: bus, PO, pub, shop, tel
South Cave: bus, PO, pub, shop, takeaway food, tel
Newbald: bus, PO, pub, shop, takeaway food, tel
Goodmanham: pub, refreshments, tel
Market Weighton: bus, PO, pub, shops (inc. outdoor equipment), café, takeaway food, tel, wc
Nunburnholme: tel
Millington: PO, pub (not open weekday lunchtimes), shop, tel
Huggate: pub (not open weekday lunchtimes), tel
Fridaythorpe: bus, café, PO, pub, shop, tel
Thixendale: café, PO, pub, shop, tel
Wharram le Street: bus, PO, café, shop, tel
Wintringham: PO, shop, tel
Sherburn: bus, PO, pub, shop, tel
Ganton: bus, pub, tel
Muston: bus, PO, pub, shop, tel
Filey: all facilities

## Useful addresses and telephone numbers

Countryside Commission, John Dower House, Crescent Place, Cheltenham, Glos, GL50 3RA. Tel. Cheltenham (0242) 521381.

*The landmark church and spire of St Nicholas, Ganton.*

Countryside Commission, Yorkshire and Humberside Region, 8a Otley Road, Leeds, LS6 2AD. Tel. Leeds (0532) 742935.

Flamborough Headland Heritage Coast Project, 4/6 Victoria Road, Bridlington, Humberside. Tel. Bridlington (0262) 678967. Or, from May Bank Holiday weekend, Heritage Centre, South Landing, Flamborough, Humberside. Tel. Bridlington (0262) 850819.

Humberside County Council, County Hall, Beverley, North Humberside, HU17 9XA. Tel. Hull (0482) 867131. (The council's Technical Services Department produces leaflets describing a series of circular walks in the Yorkshire Wolds. It is responsible for the section in Humberside (Hessle–Thixendale.)

North Yorkshire County Council, Highways and Transportation Department, Area Office, Southgate, Pickering, North Yorkshire, YO18 8BL. Tel. Pickering (0751) 72031. (Responsible for the North Yorkshire section of the Wolds Way.)

Ordnance Survey, Romsey Road, Maybush, Southampton SO9 4DH. Tel. Southampton (0703) 792792.

Ramblers' Association, 1/5 Wandsworth Road, London, SW8 2XX. Tel. London (071) 582 6878. (National campaigning body for walkers' rights; has an East Yorkshire and Derwent Area group that takes a keen interest in all Wolds Way matters; and publishes the excellent Ramblers' yearbook and accommodation guide.)

Scarborough Borough Council, Scarborough TIC, St Nicholas Cliff, Scarborough, YO11 2EP. (Has many free leaflets/programmes of attractions and events, plus accommodation in the Filey/Scarborough area.)

## Nearby places of interest

*Bempton Cliffs* Chalk precipice 440 ft (134 metres) high, an RSPB reserve where thousands of guillemots, razorbills, puffins, kittiwakes, fulmars, gannets, shags and cormorants nest.

*Beverley* The Minster (*c.* 1420) is one of Europe's most beautiful churches. There is also the Museum of Army Transport.

*Bridlington* A traditional seaside resort with some sophisticated modern attractions, such as 'Leisure World', a vast indoor pool including a surf machine. Also, Bayle Gate Museum in the Old Town is full of antiques, and there is an interesting harbour museum.

*Burton Agnes* A splendid late-Elizabethan mansion between Bridlington and Driffield. Has one of Yorkshire's most celebrated ghosts. Also, there are paintings by Gainsborough, Pissarro and Renoir, plus attractive gardens.

*Flamborough Head* Flamborough (derived from the 'flame' of beacons) is the best-preserved chalk headland in Britain. The breathtaking sea cliffs, at their highest point, are double the height of York Minster and since 1979 a 12-mile (19-km) stretch from Sewerby Steps to Black Cliff Nab, Speeton, has been defined as a Heritage Coast.

*Hull* The Docks Museum tells the story of the port's whaling and fishing history; there is also a well-preserved 'Old Town', where the home of the slavery abolitionist William Wilberforce is a museum.

*North York Moors Railway* A scenic 18-mile (29-km) line built by George Stephenson from Pickering to Goathland. It is a good way to see the National Park and well worth a detour.

*Scarborough* Noisy but, in places, elegant seaside resort with an interesting Norman castle, the grave of Anne Brontë in St Mary's churchyard, and an intriguing hologram exhibition.

*Sewerby* Sewerby Hall, a couple of miles north of Bridlington, has a collection of memorabilia from Amy Johnson, the Hull-born aviation pioneer. There is also a model village.

*Skidby Windmill* Said to be the best surviving tower mill in England, it is a prominent landmark to the south of Beverley.

*Sledmere* Home of the Sykes family, the biggest landowners in the Yorkshire Wolds and also the people responsible for converting it from a vast sheep walk to prime arable land. The original Tudor building was replaced by today's structure, a splendid Queen Anne house.

*York* Specialises in 'wet weather' attractions, such as the Railway Museum, Jorvik Centre, Castle Museum, Yorkshire Museum, and York Minster, its south transept and famous rose window now beautifully restored after the 1984 fire.

## Bibliography

There is a price to pay for the Yorkshire Wolds' unspoilt beauty and low profile among coach tour operators: unlike the North York Moors or the Yorkshire Dales, which both seem to support publishing empires, there are comparatively few books available about the Wolds, and most of the best are out of print. The following (far from complete) list will provide some suggestions for further reading for those whose appetite is whetted by a week rambling in the Wolds or just an evening spent leafing through this book.

*The gate to Sledmere Church, situated a few miles east of the Wolds Way.*

## Walking guides

Eastwood, Geoff, *Walking in East Yorkshire* (published by G. Eastwood, 60 Front St, Lockington, Driffield, North Humberside): a series of interesting rambles in the Wolds by an architect of the Wolds Way and leading authority on the area.

Humberside County Council, *Walks on the Northern Yorkshire Wolds* and *Walks on the Southern Yorkshire Wolds* (from local bookshops, TIC's or the council's Technical Services Department, County Hall, Beverley, HU17 9XA): two packs of laminated cards describing a series of excellent circular walks that have been specially waymarked. Also *A walk along the tracks – The Hudson Way* (a pack on the disused railway line); Countryside Explorer Packs for Beverley District and East Yorkshire District (two packs for the area). These include cards on places of interest, history and heritage, short and long walks, motoring and cycle trails, and disused railway lines.

Killick, Alan, *The Hull Countryway* (Lockington): describes the 51-mile (82-km) footpath around Hull, plus 14 smaller circular walks off the route.

Rubinstein, David, *The Wolds Way* (Dalesman Books, 1979): the original guide to the long-distance footpath by one of the area's most prominent campaigners for ramblers' rights. But the route is different from that described in this book.

Wallis, R., *The Minster Way* (Lockington): a guide to the 50-mile (80-km) footpath starting at Beverley Minster, crossing the Wolds and finishing at York Minster, plus some circular off-path walks.


## General guide books

Allison, K. J., *The East Riding of Yorkshire Landscape* (Hodder & Stoughton, 1976): the definitive guide to the evolution of the Wolds landscape and the history of people in the Wolds.

Arnold, Sylvia, M., *Wild Flowers of the Yorkshire Wolds* (Hutton Press, 1985): an interesting handbook to the flora of chalk landscape, with particular reference to many sites in the countryside through which the Wolds Way passes.

Elliot, Stephen C., *Bird Watching in East Yorkshire, The Humber and Teesmouth* (Hutton Press, 1989): guide to species and bird watching sites in the Humber, Wolds and along the coast.

Gower, Ted, *Filey* (Dalesman Books, 1977): a short guide to the town that lies at the end of the Wolds Way, its fishing community and places of interest.

Pevsner, Nikolaus, *Buildings of England. Yorkshire: York and the East Riding* (Penguin, 1972): the standard reference work to architecture of the area, it is especially illuminating on parish churches throughout the Wolds. Essential reading for all interested in the built environment.

Waites, Bryan, *Exploring the Yorkshire Wolds* (Dalesman Books, 1984): pocket gazetteer to the towns, villages and interesting features of East Yorkshire.

Wright, Geoffrey N., *The East Riding* (Batsford, 1976): an affectionate portrait of the area.

## Fiction

Holtby, Winifred, *Anderby Wold* (Virago Press, 1981): the East Riding's own novelist started her regrettably short writing career with this excellent portrait of life in the Yorkshire Wolds, set around Rudston, near Bridlington.

## Ordnance Survey Maps covering the Wolds Way

Landranger Maps (scale 1:50 000): 100, 101, 106, 107

Pathfinder Maps (scale: 1:25 000): 624 (TA08/09/18)
    644 (SE87/97), 645 (TA07/17), 656 (SE86/96),
    666 (SE85/95), 675 (SE84/94), 686 (SE83/93),
    695 (SE82/92), 696 (TA02/12)

Motoring Maps (scale 1:250 000): Reach the Wolds Way using Routemaster Maps 5, 'Northern England' and 6, 'East Midlands and Yorkshire'.

144